The Stories Children Tell

Making Sense of the Narratives of Childhood

Susan Engel

page 173: From *An American Childhood* by Annie Dillard. Copyright ©
1987. Reprinted by permission of HarperCollins. **pages 145–146:** From
WAYS WITH WORDS by Shirley Brice Heath. Copyright © 1983. Reprinted
with the permission of Cambridge University Press. **page 77:** Excerpts
from "Girl" from AT THE BOTTOM OF THE RIVER by Jamaica Kincaid.
Copyright © 1978, 1983 by Jamaica Kincaid. Reprinted by permission of
Farrar, Straus & Giroux, Inc. **pages 104–106:** From SAVAGE INEQUALITIES
by Jonathan Kozol. Copyright © 1991 by Jonathan Kozol. Reprinted by
permission of Crown Publishers, Inc. **page 176:** William Carlos Williams:
The Collected Poems of William Carlos Williams, 1909–1939, vol. I. Copyright 1938 by New Directions Publishing Corp. Reprinted by permission of
New Directions Publishing Corp. **pages 188–189:** From SPEAK, MEMORY
by Vladimir Nabokov. Copyright © 1967 by Vladimir Nabokov. Reprinted
by permission of Vintage Books, a Division of Random House, Inc.

Cover photo: Ellen Denuto/Photonica

Library of Congress Cataloging–in–Publication Data

Engel, Susan.
    The stories children tell : making sense of the narratives of
childhood / Susan Engel.
       p.   cm.
    Includes bibliographical references and index.
    ISBN 0–7167–2382–4
    ISBN 0–7167–3433–8 (pbk.)
    1. Symbolism (Psychology) in children. 2. Storytelling ability in
children. I. Title.
    BF723.S94E54   1994
    155.4′136—dc20

                  94–38217
                   CIP

Printed in the United States of America
First printing, 1999

For Jake, Will, and Sam—
my favorite storytellers

Contents

Preface

The stories we tell and listen to shape who we are. They give body to our own experience and take us beyond the confines of everyday life—into the past, the future, the might be. Without living in a world of stories, children can never attain full literacy. Between the ages of 1 and 8, children travel an extraordinary path, from uttering their first words to becoming complex and sometimes avid storytellers.

This book is the story of children's stories. How do children learn to tell stories? What uses does storytelling serve for young children? What do their stories mean, and how are they put together? By the time a child is 8 or 9 she may well have lost that vibrant ability to make up stories and recount experiences. Why does that happen so often, and what can prevent it from happening?

Perhaps it is because I am a developmental psychologist that I believe my own love of stories began early in life. As a young child I had not one or two imaginary friends, but, so the story goes, a cast of thousands; adults wandering by my room would hear all manner of characters talking about their lives. As a teenager, this penchant for stories parlayed itself into a theater workshop I ran for young children, who generated from personal stories all the skits and plays we put on. Much later, when I was in graduate school, one of my first research projects was on the acquisition of first words. But somehow, before I knew it, I was paying as much attention to the stories the mother and child were telling together as I was to individual word meanings. This work evolved into a focus on the social construction of children's memory. But, again, it dawned on me as I immersed myself in the transcripts of mothers and children that what was really meaningful and exciting about their talk was that they were constructing stories together.

My early experiences teaching children convinced me that to get to know a child you must listen attentively to her stories and invite her to tell you more. It is remarkable how complex and dense with meaning a young child's story can be, filled with intriguing clues for the psychological investigator and at the same time appearing so simple, organic, and spontaneous. Children's stories are a contagious passion. My sister came running over to me the other day with words scribbled hastily on a paper towel, recording her 2 year old's first story: "I didn't stay up early tonight. I stayed up good and a half and a six and a Tuesday."

Once you have opened your ears to the power and pervasiveness of stories in the lives and language of young children, you see how remarkably compelling they are, both as phenomena to be explored in their own right and as a way of understanding how young minds comprehend and construct themselves and the world around them. The key is to delve into children's narratives for information and meaning without losing one's appreciation for their beauty and communicative force—to learn how to look at them closely but still really listen to them.

In 1981, when I began graduate school, few people thought toddlers' stories were vital to psychological and social development. Now children's narratives are of tremendous interest and excitement among research psychologists. A great deal has been learned about the logic of children's stories, how to interpret the meanings of a given child's stories, and how children of different ages tell stories. But these strands of information have not been woven together to give us an accessible, cohesive picture of the range of this dynamic process. I wrote this book to weave together the strands and to integrate threads I felt were missing: the role of aesthetics in shaping young children's stories, the development of a personal narrative voice, and the role of that voice in constructing a self through stories.

In this book I explore why children tell stories, the many uses stories serve for children, and what kinds of stories they tell. I believe that one's sense of destination shapes the journey—what your concept of a story is will drive what you can learn about young children's narrative activity, and so I examine some of the prevalent theoretical frameworks within which people have studied children's narratives. I describe the origins of storytelling in the first years of life, focusing on what I believe are the two primary sites of narrative development: reminiscing with parents and symbolic play. I argue that once the cognitive and linguistic rudiments are in place by approximately 4 years of age, the most interesting developmental changes have to do with the emergence of a child's personal narrative voice. Underlying all this is my conviction that the reason stories are both pervasive and central during childhood is that through our stories we construct ourselves.

Writing this book was a true pleasure. Of course, I couldn't have done it without the voices of others. Let me thank some of them:

My conversations with Jerome Bruner inspired me. I am indebted to him for his generous help and encouragement during the early phase of this endeavor.

Discussions with friends and colleagues helped me enormously both in style and substance. Their knowledge, interest, criticisms, and questions are part of the fabric of this book. In particular, I thank Jaine Strauss, Laurie Heatherington, Karen Levine, John Dore, Steve Dollinger, Eileen Anderson, Amy Eckhardt, Mary Mullen, and the students in my seminar, "Narratives of Childhood." I thank Jacqueline Sachs for her thoughtful comments on an earlier draft. Audrey Herbst was a delightful and attentive caretaker of all kinds of details regarding the preparation of this manuscript. My thanks go also to Mary Louise Byrd for her careful work on the last stretch.

I thank Herman Engel for being a deep well of quotes, ideas, and loving interest; Kathy Engel and Jenno Topping for total support always; and Tinka Topping, my biggest champion and a wonderful colleague. My deepest admiration and appreciation go to my friend and colleague Margery Franklin. Her comments and suggestions for this book, as for all my work, have been illuminating, detailed, and substantive.

It is hard to put into words the profound and exuberant gratitude I feel for my editor, Jonathan Cobb. I couldn't have written this book without him, and I wouldn't have wanted to. I have learned tremendous amounts from him, and I deeply treasure our friendship.

I love to talk. My husband, Tom Levin, always says actions speak louder than words. True enough, his quiet but constant support and encouragement of this project spoke volumes of his pleasure and confidence in my work. I thank him for endless and wonderful love.

1

The World of Children's Stories

Every work is a stepping stone to a personal confession.

*You are Running River, and I am Hawk Eye. Let's say
you were sitting in the longhouse, and I heard a bear
coming up. So I jumped out from behind a tree, and I
speared that bear with my tomahawk. And then you
cooked the meat over the fire. Then Chief Sitting Bull
played on the drum and we had a ceremony. And I was
the hero because I killed the bear. And I got an extra
feather for my headdress.*

Every story a child tells, acts out through play, or writes
contributes to a self-portrait—a portrait that he can look at,
refer to, think about, and change, a portrait others can use to
develop an understanding of the storyteller. Each time a child
describes an experience he or someone else has had, he constructs part of his past, adding to his sense of who he is and
conveying that sense to others. Each time a child makes up a
story about something that might have happened to himself or
to another, he expands his world. The stories we tell, whether

they are about real or imagined events, convey our experience, our ideas, a dimension of who we are. It is through telling stories that children develop a personal voice, a way of communicating their unique experience and view of the world.

Told by a 5 year old to his mother in the midst of playing a game of "Indian" with her, the story about the bear is the kind an adult might easily overlook. Though not uncommon, much of interest lies behind it. Who is he in the story, and what do the events described reveal about his thoughts and experiences? How did he choose those particular details, and what determined the organization of his story? In addition to what the story can tell us about the teller, it does something important for him. In telling his mother this story, he presents himself as the hero, brave and capable, an honored member of the group. He has painted a portrait of himself.

This example captures the kind of story children often tell while playing. But as the next example shows, children reveal themselves through other kinds of stories as well, this one written by a first grader:

The walking eyeball

The eyeball was a yoyo. He ran, yoyo yoyo. The eyeball was with his little brother. And he did a rolypoly bunk. And he squirted a rock out of the hose. There was a windstorm. They didn't blow over from the windstorm. And they were holding on to their feet-hands. He kicked another eyeball. He thought it was a ball. He was rolling in circles. He went home and he saw the sun.

This story, more arresting and clearly original than the first with its vivid use of language and striking choice of characters and events, also invites questions about the story, the storyteller, and their relation: Is the author a 6 year old or the eyeball, and if so, why an eyeball? What do the dramatic events in the story suggest? Why does it end the way it does? Where and how did this author learn to weave together description and drama?

We tend to assume that only the stories we read by accomplished authors are complex, replete with meaning, and worthy of close analysis. We often dismiss children's stories as simply cute and rather transparent, limited in meaning and complexity. They can seem charming to us because of their simplicity, their outrageousness, or their odd construction. They can seem obvious when we think the child is communicating a thinly veiled fear or wish. But children's stories are often complex in style and voice, construction, and content. What a child's story means can be as interesting, though different, a question as what *Anna Karenina* means. If we listen closely, it offers us a new way of looking at and understanding children. Children's stories can be vital to us as parents, teachers, and researchers because they give us insight into how children of different ages experience the world, and how a specific child thinks and feels. And as an increasing number of researchers are discovering, stories and storytelling are vital to children themselves and to their development.

This book is about how young children go about making up and telling stories. It is about the content and construction of their stories. It describes the paths by which children move from the barest one-word references to events from their past to the long, complex fantasies of preschoolers at play. And it is about the ways in which the stories that pervade children's lives contribute to the child's burgeoning sense of self and developing relationship with the world.

The Pervasiveness of Narratives

◆

A child's world is filled with stories. Long before children can recount their own tales, they hear stories told to and around them. If we listen to those stories and attend to them rather than treating them as background noise, we begin to appreciate their frequency in the child's life. Babies are surrounded by the stories parents, siblings, and friends tell to one another, and to them, a captive audience. By the time children are 2 and 3 years old, they begin adding their own voices to the stories that surround them.

If you spend a morning with some children at home or in a day-care setting, you will hear a multitude of narratives. Children will tell stories to one another, to their teacher, and to themselves. They will tell formulaic stories and wild rambling stories. They will tell complete stories and fragments of stories. They will tell stories about things that have happened to them, things that have happened to other people, and things that couldn't possibly happen to anyone. A great deal of their play is either based on an implicit narrative or generates a narrative in the form of a line-by-line account of their actions. If you offer to tell a story, or even just begin telling one, you will find yourself surrounded by eager, open faces, ready to hear your story. As children get older, they hear and tell an even wider variety of stories, including written stories, novels, and formal reports of actual events.

As one gauge of the extent of early storytelling, developmental psychologists Peggy Miller and Lois Sperry tape-recorded the talk of mothers and toddlers in their homes at the end of each day. They discovered that, on average, for each hour of tape-recorded conversations, almost nine stories were told, often by the parent to the child but sometimes by the child. Although no one has systematically assessed the pervasiveness of narratives in the young child's life, if you take all of the research on narrative and compare the reports with one another, you find wonderfully robust evidence for a great variety and quantity of stories that children are exposed to and engage in telling from a very early age. And the narrative experience doesn't end with childhood. In a college class on language development, I asked students how many stories they told in a typical day. Many of them said none or perhaps one. Then I asked them to keep a record for twenty-four hours of the stories they told. They all arrived at the next class session surprised with their own results. They said they had told anywhere from five to thirty-eight stories in the day, and felt that, if anything, they had missed some.

Why are we likely to underestimate the number and variety of stories we tell? Perhaps it is because they are so much a part of our lives that we don't realize their extent and because our first response is typically to think only of well-formed stories with clear plots and identifiable authors. In everyday practice we only approximate this narrative model, however, and end up telling a lot of stories that contain ingredients of this model but don't strictly meet its criteria. Many more narratives are embedded, often unnoticed, in our everyday activity than the well-formed stories we may tell to someone.

Not only are narratives pervasive in terms of the quantity and variety that unfold in the daily life of many children and adults, narratives pervade the inner life as well. Toddlers and preschoolers often construct monologues while playing, going to sleep, and spending time alone. Then, as they get older, their spoken monologues are replaced by dreams, daydreams, and unspoken soliloquies. The stories we tell ourselves, aloud or silently, play a vital role in shaping what we feel, think, and know about our lives.

What is it about stories that accounts for their pervasiveness? Surely, an activity that is so much a part of our lives serves some significant purpose, both in the prosaic everyday aspects of experience and in our more infrequent moments of crisis and transformation. Narratives, for one thing, share a characteristic of language more generally; they give us a new way in which to experience life. As the Russian psychologist Alexander Luria pointed out so eloquently, the acquisition of language gives us a second world, beyond the world of immediate action:

> In the absence of words, humans would have to deal only with those things which they could perceive and manipulate directly. With the help of language, they can deal with things which they have not perceived even indirectly and with things which were part of the experience of earlier generations. Thus, the word adds another dimension to the world of humans. . . . Animals have only one world, the world of objects and situations which can be perceived by the senses. Humans have a double world.

If Luria is right, and I believe he is, then stories are the second level of experience, par excellence. Living in both worlds, the world of action and objects and the world of stories, is what makes human experience distinctive. Children who have acquired language, like adults, shift back and forth in this double world, each world shaping the other, their stories organizing their perceptions of actions and objects, their perceptions of actions and objects informing their stories.

For my son Jake, every scar on his father's body contains a story. When Jake was 8 years old he went to spend a few days with his grandfather in Vermont. When his grandfather brought Jake home, he told me that Jake had been regaling him with stories Tom, his father, had recounted of childhood mishaps, including falling off a bike and getting a concussion, walking into a glass door and needing forty-three stitches, and, when a young man, getting knifed while driving a cab in Boston. According to his grandfather, Jake then said, "Boy, I sure hope some things like that start happening to me soon." When his grandfather asked why, he replied instantly, "So that I have some stories to tell my kids and my grandkids, of course!"

Stories reflect multiple strands and levels of our experience. I have just told you a story: about a story my father told me, about some stories his grandson had told him. The grandson's stories were based on the stories he had been told by his father. And my son's main point was that one value in having interesting experiences is that you have good stories to tell in the future. Although not all children would articulate the need to experience things in order to be able to tell stories about them someday, this anecdote about Jake underscores how important storytelling can be to young children. It suggests that already by the age of 8, children have some implicit sense (or, in Jake's case, an explicit sense) of the two stages on which we live our lives: experience and the retelling of that experience.

Jake, like many 8 year olds, already has his own firm idea of what experiences make good story material. He already has a strong enough narrative framework in his mind that he can repeat, fairly accurately, stories that have been told to him. Through his retelling of these stories to his grandfather, he not only expresses himself but coordinates several different relationships and types of information. He uses those stories about his father to know better what kind of guy his father is and what kind of life he has had. He tells about it to his grandfather as a way of letting his grandfather know what is important to him about his father and as a way of being close to his grandfather. And finally he thinks about wanting stories of his own to tell as a way of projecting into the future what kind of person he will be.

The Narrative Revolution

◆

Despite their centrality in children's lives, stories and story-telling have, until recently, received remarkably little attention from psychologists. If many parents and some teachers tend to dismiss young children's stories as simply cute, developmental psychologists traditionally have either not looked at children's stories at all or tended to look through stories for information about a child's level of, for example, cognitive development.

Research on children's development has often directed our attention to what children do rather than what they say (researchers typically observe, record, and code behaviors: their gestures, performance on various tasks, solutions of problems). This is due in part to the predominance of behaviorism in mainstream psychology during most of this century, which posits that psychologists should concern themselves with people's actions rather than their thoughts and words. Even when researchers are interested in what children say, it is often only because they want to know what children of a given age are capable of: Can they think logically? Can they sequence events accurately? Can they remember a list of items?

During the 1960s and 1970s, as psychologists began to use the computer as a model for the mind and developed new methods of research, an emphasis on the way we think was reintroduced into psychology. Research on information processing described human thought and resulting behavior in terms of decision trees, flowcharts, and various other computer processes. These accounts describe the young child's mind as a series of processing rules, nested in ways that allow the child to build increasingly complex strategies as a function of his or her daily experiences.

In recent years, some of the ideas that grew out of information processing have led a growing number of psychologists to look at both children's and adults' stories in a provocative new way. Stories, they argue, are not only something we tell at a party, in school, or on stage, nor are they simply so many signs of developmental competence. We also think through stories. In a spate of recent books, cognitive psychologists have suggested that narratives are the form in which we organize experience, and that stories, or the outlines of stories, guide not only our memory but also our experience of what is happening and what may happen in the future. That is, we take in fragments of information and organize them in a narrative form: first this happened, then so and so did this, then that happened over there.

This renewed emphasis on how we think has allowed us to take a fresh look at children's experiences, at what children say, and at the role of meaning in guiding how we think. After all, stories are told by people to people. They reflect the values, interpretations, and ideas of narrator and listener. Jerome Bruner has argued that while we may learn about the physical world through logical rules and abstract principles, we learn about the social world through narratives. As children take in the stories they hear all around them, they also take in a particular interpretation of events and experience. People experience their lives as a series of overlapping and fluctuating stories. The beauty of this idea is that it helps explain how children become integrated with their culture. Listening to and telling stories are cultural activities. As children learn the story form, they also learn about their culture. In turn, through stories, aspects of their culture shape the way they think about and remember experiences.

Stories and the Self

◆

If it is true that narratives are the fundamental form in which we structure and communicate social experience, how do they affect us both day by day and over the span of many years? Over the course of our lives, we continually build a sense of self through our stories of personal experience. We remember events and occasions and repeat those experiences to ourselves and to others in a story form. We do this with exciting and important events, the kinds that make "good story material," and we do it with the banal everyday experiences of life as well. Take these three simple examples, from a family dinner table conversation.

(Mother to one of the children)
    Guess what happened while you were away? You know how the cat was missing? Well, we went over to Lucy's house to call for her. Even though she had been gone so long, we thought maybe if she was still some-where around and she heard our voices she might come back. And we went over there and called and called, and Sam called out, "Peep, it's me, Sam. And you're Peep. Remember me, the little kid who pets you all the time?" But she didn't come, and so finally we went home and

Sam was really sad that we hadn't found her. And guess what? A few hours later Lucy called us and told us Peep was at the door! She had come home because she had heard Sam calling for her! After all those days!

To the people in this family, this is an exciting experience. The children love their cat dearly, and Sam, the protagonist, is both amazed and gratified by his role in bringing home the lost cat, and the parents are deeply touched by what the event reveals about Sam's attachment to his pet. The story crystallizes these personally meaningful aspects for storyteller and listener alike. It's a story they may repeat again and again, and some day the children may repeat it to their children. As time passes, each family member may develop his or her unique version of the story.

Less involved events are also related in a story form.

(One of the children to the whole family)
    "Today at camp I fell down in the grass. And the grass cut my leg. It really hurt. And Kerry put some first-aid cream on it."
    (The mother looks at this child for a moment, silently acknowledging his story, and then gives the youngest child, a 3 year old, a chance to contribute a story by asking)
    "And what did you do at your camp today?"
    "Played. And Lisa sang us a song."

The first child tells a short but coherent story about what happened at camp. The 3 year old gives the simplest of narrative responses: It has the elements of narrative without being a full-fledged story. Still, it has hints of things to come, a building block toward the child's ability to order experience and convey it to others within a story form.

Over time, some important stories will remain vivid, and the everyday ones will fade or become merged with others until they simply form a general impression of experience at a given time in one's life. The story about the lost cat may remain significant for one member of the family (perhaps Sam) and not for the others. The second and third stories may be forgotten by all but blended into the two children's narratives of what their childhood summer camp was like. What makes a story important is highly individual and subject to complex psychological forces. Sometimes an event that seems totally trivial to the audience remains indelibly imprinted in the mind of the storyteller.

Children not only tell stories of actual experience to build a sense of self, they also invent stories about things that might happen, that couldn't possibly happen, that they wish would happen, or that they hope fervently will never happen.

Once there was a dog. He loved kids. He was very happy. His name was Ike. He saw this black thing and it was a ship. So he climbed on the ship and the ship took him to Africa. He saw lots and lots of lions and bears and tigers and monkeys. He ran away and he went in the bushes and he saw a bushman, and the land of Africa. Then he got back on the ship and the ship took him home and he saw his mommy. The end.

Invention is as central as recall in the construction of stories, and of the self, regardless of whether the story uses specific recollections. This 5 year old has invented a story about what might happen, but it includes personal material as well: He does have a dog named Ike, he has been learning about Africa, and he was very concerned at the time about feeling close to his mother.

Children weave together real concerns, real experiences, and fantasy to convey what is important to them. This is not peculiar to children; as the Spanish film director Luis Buñuel once said:

> Our imagination, and our dreams, are forever invading our memories; and since we are all apt to believe in the reality of our fantasies, we end up transforming our lies into truths. Of course, fantasy and reality are equally personal, and equally felt, so their confusion is a matter of only relative importance.

It's not just what we remember that shapes our experience and our sense of who we are. It is also how we remember. Do we remember isolated images, fragments of dialogue, or complex events in sequence? Do we remember in detail or recall only the bare bones? Do we remember the feelings associated with an experience or just the actions? Or do we remember in a way that captures not only what happened but how it felt?

In a recording of adults reminiscing about their childhoods, one man talked about how severe his father was, how scary the punishments were. But, he mused, he could never remember what he had done to trigger or warrant the punishment; he could only remember what his father did in reaction to the forgotten deed. In reconstructing his memory of his experiences, in telling stories of his childhood, the man sifted out his own actions and remembered what was for him the powerful part of the experience, his father's wrath. In editing like that, he reveals the conscious personal meaning of the remembered experience: that his father's wrath far outweighed his misdeeds.

Whether a particular story is remembered or not, the act of telling a story is always important to the developing child, because in the telling the child is both practicing telling stories and building up an inventory of stories that contribute to a life story and a self-representation. Who knows how he will use, save, savor, and blend these stories in the future. Why does that matter? Because to a great extent we are the stories we tell, and our memories of personal experiences are what give us a history and a sense of who we are—past, present, and future.

Storytelling and Literacy

Storytelling not only contributes to self-representation, the developing logic in a child's experience, and integration with one's surrounding culture but also seems to play an important role in literacy development. In *The Meaning Makers,* Gordon Wells summarizes his fifteen-year study of a group of children living in England. It is one of the most ingenious and comprehensive collections of children's language that we have. One of Wells's primary interests was in finding the roots of literacy and discovering the links, if any, among home life, the individual child, school experience, and school success. Literacy, he discovered, is at the heart of school success and originates during the early years.

What this study clearly demonstrates is that it is growing up in a literate family environment, in which reading and writing are naturally occurring, daily activities, that gives children a particular advantage when they start their formal education. And of all the activities that were characteristic of such homes, *it was the sharing of stories that we found to be most important.*

Many of us now know, through books, magazine articles, and radio and television ads, that it is good to read to our children. But what Wells is saying is that reading is only one part of literacy. Telling and hearing stories is just as important as sitting down and reading sentences in a book. He includes one important caveat: The kinds of stories children tell must be listened to and appreciated so that children can make use of those stories when they need to make the leap into literacy.

Storytelling and Development

We may ask, what are the roots of this clearly essential human process? Children's ability to tell stories does not, of course, arrive full-blown. One of the most fascinating questions about children's narratives is how they first emerge and begin to develop.

Children learn the story form (and the large number of variations on the form) at a remarkably early age. And they do so with such ease that it seems completely untutored and natural. It is natural, but it isn't untutored. As with language learning itself, research has shown that a great deal of parental input and shaping contributes to the child's developing the capacity for storytelling. Children's narrative style and ability reflect individual, familial, and community values and ways of telling. This tutoring is not usually explicit or formal but, rather, is enmeshed in the casual conversations that children hear and participate in.

In the beginning stages of their storytelling, children often only offer germs of stories (we discuss this further in Chapter 5); but as they get older, their stories become structurally more complex, longer, and more conventionally dramatic. Note the difference between these stories, one told by a 2 year old, the other by a 5 year old. Each is about a personal experience, but they are different in length, structure, and style. Moreover, the first is typical of a toddler's story in that it is told to a parent, whereas the 5 year old is much more likely to engage in storytelling with a peer.

A 2 year old says to her mother:

We went trick and treating. I got candy. A big red lolly-pop and I lost my hat.

A 5 year old says to his friend:

Ya know what? Ya know what? We had a raccoon on our porch. A big, huge raccoon. It was in the tree and he was trying to eat the bird food. And we wanted to kill it, but my Mom didn't want our Dad to kill it. But he killed it anyway. And there was raccoon blood all over the porch.

By the time children are 3 years old, many of their stories will have something like a beginning, a middle, and an end. They will remember stories they have heard and describe their own experiences in a story form. By the time they are 5, children have distinctive personal styles of storytelling. They will also know the story custom of their particular community and have some idea about what makes a story a story. By the age of 8, most children can tell several different types of stories upon request and can accurately relate complex events.

Narratives and Stories

◆

To appreciate the development of children's storytelling it's important to have some sense of what a story is and what it is not. Most of us know a story when we hear it. A story, first of all, describes something that has happened, is happening, or will happen. It includes some kind of event. Events involve people, places, and actions. Someone does something, and it happens somewhere. Moreover, all events happen within a time frame and unfold over time. Thus in most stories there is some feeling, explicit or implicit, of sequence. First one thing happens, then another. They are related either because one thing leads to another (I ran for the ball, then I slipped, then I broke my arm) or because several things happen that, when described together, reveal a common theme (It was raining, I felt sad, I broke my favorite bowl, my dog ran away; this was a misery day).

A 5 year old recalls a football game played with some other children and some grown-ups:

We really kicked butts out there. When I jumped on Jon, it was like a snake in cement. I wouldn't let him go. Then I grabbed the football. I was like a snake swallowing a frog. The football was the frog.

This is a story because it relates a series of actions over time. There is a protagonist, who is also the narrator. There is a large event—the football game—and within its context a specific event, wresting the ball from a grown-up. There is a place (out there) and an implied time frame (something in the immediate past). There are actions (jumping on Jon, grabbing the ball, holding it) that, when told together, relate a meaning (I was a tough football player). This particular story has little in the way of dramatic tension, a high point, or a resolution, qualities that we associate with good adult literature. It does not have subtle characterization. It is, however, a vivid recounting of something in this little boy's experience. It describes his experience in a unique way. It is not classic literature, but it does contain the rudiments of a story.

The most important thing about a story is that by relating people, actions, objects, place, and time, the storyteller conveys meaning. Part of that meaning is conveyed by the story's perspective or point of view. Events are seen through someone's eyes. In the 5 year old's football story, the boy's meaning revolves around a sense of personal triumph. In children's stories particularly, where sequence and plot are not always clearly developed, the key to understanding, appreciating, and responding to the story often lies in understanding the meaning, the perspective of the narrator.

In *Aspects of the Novel*, E. M. Forster aptly describes what happens when we disembed the temporal sequence of events from the fuller meaning of a narrative: "When we isolate the story like this from the nobler aspects through which it moves, and hold it out on the forceps,—wriggling and interminable, the naked worm of time—it presents an appearance that is both unlovely and dull."

The same is true of children's stories. Stripped of their evoked, often nuanced meanings, their perspective, viewed simply in terms of plot or sequence of told events, they not only appear unlovely and dull, they lose their psychological significance. This poses a special challenge when trying to uncover what is going on, what is developing in children's storytelling. We must identify patterns, uncover predictable and reliable structures or processes, and at the same time attend to the often subtle and idiosyncratic qualities that make narratives so interesting and powerful in the first place.

Some researchers believe a story has to include clues as to why the story is being told in order for it to qualify as a story. For instance, is the storyteller trying to teach her friends a moral lesson, is she trying to explain how her shoes came to be so muddy, is she retelling the plot of a favorite book? These clues may appear by way of the context (a child talking to a circle of friends or responding to the request of an adult), or they may appear as a comment within the story itself (". . . which is why people who brag end up losing . . .").

Most of the stories related in this book involve one or two storytellers who know they are telling a story (at the dinner table, at show and tell, in the block corner). But if we're to understand the early development of storytelling, we need to cast a wider net. Here a distinction between narrative and story can be helpful.

A narrative is an account of experiences or events that are temporally sequenced and convey some meaning. A narrative can be of an imagined event or a lived everyday event. But, unlike a story, which is told or communicated intentionally, a narrative can be embedded in a conversation or interaction and need not be experienced as a story by the speakers ("Yeah, when Jerry and me went outside he climbed a tree and fell." "Is that when he got that gross cut on his knee?").

Children often construct narratives in the context of play or playful conversation ("I'm putting my baby to sleep.

Then she's gonna wake up and I have to give her dinner, and she's gonna cry and say, 'Mamma, Mamma.'"). These narratives may not have an explicit message, although it is almost always implicit and available for analysis. Often play narratives are constructed collaboratively. These are the narratives that are identified, lifted out, and retold as stories by a listener, a therapist, a researcher. They share characteristics with the more obvious kinds of stories, but it's worth remembering the difference. For instance, a child may be able to express complex meanings and sequences in his play with a friend and yet not be ready to construct a story on his own, at the request of an adult. A child may convey deep personal feelings about himself in a conversation with a parent about a past experience and yet not be able deliberately to create a story about those feelings to share with others. Similarly, the adult listener must sometimes weave together the narrative that seems to be buried in the flow of a child's play and conversation, much as Freud, in the guise of an archaeologist of the mind, took static buried memories and symbols and wove them together to make a narrative.

These reconstructed and interpreted narratives are different from but can be as interesting as the more cohesive stories children consciously produce. And, as we shall see, narrative fragments that can be identified in a toddler's talk contribute to that child's ability to tell stories when he is older.

While at the most general level stories pervade the lives of everyone, it is also true that for a child to feel a robust sense of power and ownership, to feel that he can tell all kinds of stories to express all kinds of meanings, he has to live in a place where people encourage him to tell stories. But this is not as simple or as common as one might think.

When you write a book you sit down and tell your story in one piece. You hope that someone will read it. Your image of the reader's response may guide you in what you put in your story and how you say it. But you have the floor. Children, on the other hand, usually just hope that they have the floor. Often they have to try and get the floor back from another child or a bossy adult. And they have to try and keep the floor, by telling an interesting and meaningful story.

A lot of the stories children tell happen within other conversations. Children have to find the right moment, not lose their train of thought, and often depend on their listener to help them build the story.

A 3 year old says "I went on a boat," and looks at you expectantly. Are you interested? Do you want to know more? Do you already know all about it? So you say, "That's nice. Tie your shoes." End of story. Or you say, "You did?" "Yeah, I went on a big boat." You show that you are interested and the story gets a little longer and more detailed. You say, "Where did you go on that boat?" "We went to Long Island. With my Mommy I went. And my Daddy." "Was it fun? Did you see the water?" "Yes, we saw the water and we saw fishes! And I ate a hot dog."

Now there's a story. But when you are 3, you often need a partner to tell a story. And what your partner does or doesn't say can have a big influence on what the story turns out to be.

Five-year-old Aron and his mother are lying in a hammock at the end of the day. Aron looks up at the trees and says, "Lots of people like to cut up God's ice-cream cones and use them for firewood." Then he stands up, balancing on the strings of the hammock, towering over his mother and says in a ferocious voice, "I am a wild Naki-Tunya!" He then leaps off the hammock and starts to swing his mother in it, and says to her, "Can string float?" His mothers responds, "Yeah. String floats." He says, "Okay, you are on a string boat."

The seeds of stories are in so much of what children say. In five minutes Aron had sent out three floaters, three possible opening narrative lines. Many openers are left undeveloped and just fade into the never-never land of possible play, possible stories. But they are sent out like signals. The sender, the child, never knows which one will turn into a full-fledged story. What will make it develop beyond a seed and become a full, cohesive story? Sometimes it's just a question of a beginning that is so interesting to the child that she develops it into a story without any prompting. Sometimes a question from another child or an adult prompts her to develop a story. Sometimes another child catches on to the idea, and adds something in a statement or question form that becomes the second line, the beginning of a collaborative story.

As these examples suggest, children have a natural delight in telling a story. Not all children have a receptive audience for their stories. But if they are given encouragement and a responsive ear, they relish in making up stories of all kinds, a process that is vital to their daily lives and overall development.

2

Why Children Tell Stories

Imagine a young boy's day:

The boy traipses out of bed and into his parents' room. "Sweetie, how did you sleep?" his mother asks. "Bad. I dreamt I had no head, and I had to pick a head from a sea of heads, and then I picked one with a hatchet in it, and then I woke up with a headache." Later, sitting at the breakfast table, he idly picks up his spoon. It becomes a pirate: "Pow. Ugh, oh, I got shot. I'll get you, you're Long John Silver. Oh, no you won't, I've got a knife. Pow, ugh."

He arrives at school and begins to tussle playfully with Carlos, his best friend. Carlos recounts a wild episode of roughhousing with his older brother: "And then I jumped on top of him, and you know what? I held down both his arms." Delighted to be included in this tale, the little boy asks eagerly,

"And did he get free?" "Nope," Carlos replies. "I held him down and I won the wrestle." Later, they are playing blocks with another child. "Let's pretend this is a space station. We can be spacemen, and I'll hand you the wood to build the new spaceship. And then you'll be the Alien. And you will come up from behind. . . ." "Yeah. And I'll shoot you with my ray gun."

Later in the day, the boy remembers that his parents are about to leave on a trip. He recalls in some detail how upset he had been the last time he was left with the baby-sitter. He imagines to himself that while his parents are away he will fall out of a tree and break his arm, and when they return they will feel horrible about it. Finally, it is dinnertime. His parents and his sisters are talking excitedly about the ups and downs of their day. He wants a chance: "You know what happened today? Jessie got stung by seven bees! And her whole face puffed up!" Everyone turns to him to ask more about the incident. In bed later, recounting the events of the day to himself in a series of stories, he remembers with glee the moment when his teacher told him how beautiful the picture he had painted was and, with some anxiety, the details of a fight he had with another friend.

Now imagine this same day without any stories, much as James Thurber, in *The Wonderful O,* imagined a world without the letter O.

The little boy wakes up and goes into his parents' room. His mother asks him how he slept. He answers briefly, "Not good." At the breakfast table he picks up the spoon, but unable to act out a story, he simply jounces it up and down. At school he and his friend roughhouse a bit and talk about how strong they are, but Carlos has no way of conveying the tussle with his brother the night before or of sharing in his friend's life outside of preschool. When they build with blocks, they direct each other ("Put that block over here." "I'm building a tall one." "This is a space station."). But without a guiding narrative framework, they cannot collaborate in a full pretend sequence.

The boy is worried about his parents' trip, but he doesn't imagine a scenario that expresses his anger and anxiety, or one that allows him at least momentarily to get back at them for leaving him. At dinner, everyone chats, but no one recounts the day's experiences, and so no one knows what happened to the other people in the family. Finally, it is bedtime, and as he goes to sleep, the boy thinks about his day and talks to himself, noting the good and uncomfortable things that happened to him and some of the feelings he had. But even though he can imagine them, even label them, without a storylike framework in which to embed them, these images and words have little order, no clear protagonist, no explicit continuity, no real drama.

This is a farfetched fantasy, of course, but as with Thurber's story, it helps one to appreciate how central stories are to almost every aspect of our daily lives. If you take a moment and try to reconstruct your day, minus any stories you heard or told to yourself or others, the day becomes pretty bare and colorless—more like a list than a full recollection. And, of course, without stories, you would not be able to carry out the task I just suggested.

But stories do more than simply add color to the day. We use stories to guide and shape the way we experience our daily lives, to communicate with other people, and to develop relationships with them. We tell stories to become part of the social world, to know and reaffirm who we are. This is particularly true for young children.

When Michael Halliday wrote *Learning How to Mean,* he gave us a new way of looking at children's language and its role in development. Halliday, a British researcher, kept a meticulous account of what his son Nigel said and heard during his first years, using the data to develop and illustrate his theory of language acquisition. He showed us that understanding what children use language for—the functions of language—can teach us the meaning of their language at different ages and can show us what aspects of language use develop over time. In its simplest form, Halliday's view is that language has two basic functions: We use language to think with (the mathetic function), and we use language to communicate (the communicative function).

This is an excellent starting point for considering the basic functions of narrative. Narratives, like language more generally, have the same overarching functions; we construct stories to think with and to communicate. These uses are not mutually exclusive. Most of the time, in fact, when we tell a story we are fulfilling both functions at once, although one may take precedence over the other. If you've already told the story about last week's fall on the stairs many times over, and you are now telling it at a gathering of friends, the social/communicative function is much more salient than any mathetic or cognitive function. On the other hand, if you're driving home from a disturbing get-together with your parents and you begin to remember an episode from your childhood, in effect telling it to yourself, the mathetic function of narrative is more at the fore than any communicative need.

Putting remembered experience into a story form allows us to think about our past, even when we have no intention of sharing those thoughts with anyone.

Halliday believes that the social function precedes the language that will fulfill that function and that the social function is most probably inborn. He used an anecdote about Nigel to demonstrate the infant's early urge to communicate and give meaning to his experience: When Nigel is 2 months old, and his father comes home, Nigel cries in a distressed way, in what Halliday interprets as the communicative, sharing mode. Halliday says that this demonstrates Nigel's impulse to share with his father his experience of having been vaccinated that day and the distress it caused him.

From current research it is now clear that infants do not recall complex episodes from their personal past, in part because without language the young infant has no means of structuring past events. It seems doubtful, then, that Nigel could, in any coherent way, reflect on his vaccination experience or have the urge to convey it. The notable thing, however, is that Halliday, like many parents in similar situations, interpreted the cry as indicative of his son's attempt to share an experience, and Halliday responded appropriately. This interpretive feedback has an important effect on the developing child. Parents' interpretations of their children's communicative intentions, in other words, help to shape what their children's intentions actually are, and in that way help to shape what functions storytelling will serve for them.

Recently I observed a 21-month-old toddler playing in a small park. His mother was watching him from a bench nearby. At one point he came over, climbed up next to her, and began talking incomprehensibly, though he spoke as if he were saying real words and real sentences. When he paused, his mother looked at him and said, "Oh, yeah? And then what happened?" As with Nigel's father, her interpretation of her son's intention was that he was trying to tell a story. And whether or not he had that in mind, her response let him know that that was what he might someday want to do: tell her a story about what happened.

Making Sense of the World

◆

A mother describes an exchange with her son:

> *Yesterday Joey was on his swing and I was lying on the grass near him, keeping him company. He started swinging higher and higher. Then he said, "What if I swing all the way around. What if I swing all the way up into the sky? What if I swing right up until I am touching the sun?" And I answered, "You better not swing all the way up into the sun. Then you will be like Icarus." There was a pause for a moment or two as he pumped back and forth, and then he said, "So, tell me about the story of this Licorice guy."*

In the light of new information, Joey immediately wants to know the story that will clarify and elaborate his understanding. At the age of 4 he already recognizes that stories can be a powerful tool for understanding the world. The roots of this recognition, however, lie much earlier in life. Imagine an infant, say, 12 months old, each day facing a bewildering morass of experiences, sensations, and activities. How is she to get a grip on the flow of experience? What must she do mentally to order and shape the onslaught of perceptions and emotions so that she can participate in the world around her in a sensible way? Developmental psychologists have been asking this question, in one form or another, for more than fifty years. Perhaps the most compelling answer, and certainly the currently dominant one, is that children organize experience into sequences; they experience the world as a series of events.

Evidence suggests that we group, categorize, and sort along different dimensions, depending on our age, our personality, the situation in which we find ourselves, and our current goal or orientation. Many psychologists have examined the ways in which abstract concepts guide our thinking (for instance, we perceive, think, and talk about a specific chair in terms of the categories of chair, furniture, inanimate objects, and the like). During the 1970s, the psychologists Roger Schank and Robert Abelson, using the computer as their model, argued that we construct specific organizational frameworks to guide our everyday functioning. They called these frameworks scripts, and suggested that we use mental scripts, rather than abstract categories, to get a grip on the flow of experience. We organize our expectations about events and our actions within those events, around central goals (eating at a restaurant, getting ready for work, and so forth). Within these goal-defined scripts we see things in terms of actors, locations, actions, and time.

Katherine Nelson took Schank and Abelson's script theory and made it explicitly developmental. She argued that children experience their day as a series of scripts, or routines; they use those routines to understand how the world works, what is going to happen when, and who is going to do what. For instance, many children have a breakfast script that helps them anticipate the sequence of morning events (first Mommy comes in and takes me out of the crib, then we get dressed, then we go into the kitchen and have juice or milk, and cereal or eggs, and then . . .).

Nelson's evidence for the primacy of scripts as an organizing tool for the child was this: When preschoolers are asked about an event in their day as if it were a specific thing that had just happened (an anecdote), often they are unable to tell you much. But when Nelson and her colleagues asked these young children to tell what usually happens during a particular activity or time in the day, the children were able to say quite a lot, narrated as a sequence of actions that take place in time and space. If, for instance, you ask a 3 year old what she had for breakfast that morning, she might just shrug her shoulders and give you a vague look, but if you ask that same child, "What do you *eat* for breakfast?" she is much more likely to give you a detailed answer.

Moreover, the child's response will likely reflect not only her general script for "eating breakfast" but some of the flexibility of mind she has acquired for changing content within certain slots. She might answer, for instance, "Oh, I have cereal and juice. And sometimes I have bacon. Or if Mommy has no cereal, then I have toast with jam." In other words, she can use her general script to sort new or varying experiences into categories that reflect the organization of events—the different people who might feed her breakfast, the different foods she might eat, and when she is older the different actions she might perform at breakfast (setting the table, buttering the toast, pouring the juice).

This view of how a child organizes information is in striking contrast to earlier views that had asserted that children organize the world right from the beginning into more ostensibly adultlike conceptual categories—foods, people, actions. These earlier psychological notions of how children organize experience tended to make children look inept (unable to answer questions about what they ate for breakfast that morning). They supported the long-standing concept of children as somewhat confused, passive creatures who did little to make sense of their daily experience. When they are asked questions based on their script knowledge instead of their knowledge of conceptual categories or their memories of specific occasions—asking "What do you eat for breakfast?"

instead of asking "Name three fruits" or "What did you eat this morning at breakfast?"—3 year olds look much more competent.

Nelson's theory emphasizes the idea that the world is experienced in socially meaningful units—event sequences— rather than as a set of perceptually based abstractions (blue things, round things, square things). Nelson, like Schank and Abelson, stresses the goal-oriented nature of our organization of life. All of us, children especially, are more likely to group things in terms of the goal they serve than in terms of some set of abstracted properties they have in common. Children are thus more likely to put things together mentally that occur together (the things that go together at lunch: sandwiches, juice, cookies, sitting at little tables, clean-up time, and the like) rather than those that can be grouped by abstract categories independent of their association with particular events (red things, things with four sides). These more abstract conceptual categories don't gain mental prominence until later in development, when children begin to function in a more purely linguistic conceptual domain. This model of how children make sense of experience, the script, looks a lot like a story, an event with actions, actors, and objects, occurring in time and space. This is no accident; scripts are narratives in germ.

The link between children's cognitive scripts and narratives was explored more fully in an extraordinary case study Nelson organized in the 1980s. For nearly two years Nelson tape-recorded the words of a little girl named Emily, as she talked herself to sleep each night from age 21 months to 3 years. One of the most interesting things about the Emily project is tnat after collecting the data Nelson invited a group of noted language and developmental researchers to analyze the transcripts, each from his or her own perspective. These data and their interpretations by a variety of researchers have become a central text in the developing body of narrative theory.

The most striking feature of the transcripts is that so much of Emily's speech occurs in a storylike form. Whether Emily is talking about things that have happened to her that day, long ago, or things that will happen to her in the future, *happen* is the operative word. Emily tells herself stories about herself. She uses this story form to make sense of the world around her and her place in it. "I 'member the . . . I went to sleep . . . and Daddy said . . . buy diapers for Stephen and Emmy . . . and buy something for Stephen plug in and say ahhh . . . and put the in . . . on Saturday go Childworld, buy diaper for Emmy."

Even when Emily gets the order wrong, or the information itself wrong, she is sequencing events, working on constructing an order to her experience. "Tomorrow, when we wake up from bed, first me and Daddy and Mommy, you, eat breakfast . . . eat breakfast, like we *usually* do, and then we're going to p-l-a-y, and then soon as Daddy comes, Carl's going to come over, and then we're going to play a little while."

Emily uses the story form to figure out who the actors are, what actions they take, and in what order these actions occur. The stories we construct not only order experience but order it in ways that are meaningful to us. When Emily puts experience into a story form in her monologues, she can thus stress the high points of the experience through her language, teasing apart the shifting and invariant aspects of certain episodes. And through her stories, she can attempt to sort through which are the essential and which the peripheral aspects of a recalled experience.

The metaphor Nelson and others often used initially to describe the relation of children's scriptlike language and the world referred to by that language was that of a square frame placed on a square piece of paper. The implication in Nelson's early script research was that there was some kind of perceptual primacy to organizing the world in terms of events; the way the child experiences the world—in terms of events and scripts—fits or matches the way the world is structured. Another version of this view is that scripts match the way people are biologically tuned to perceive the world.

There is an alternative possibility, however: that from very early on adults describe the world to young children in terms of scripts and routines. Parents narrate their children's daily lives: "Look, let's put on this pretty red coat, 'cause then we are going outside to see Ruby. And we'll take Ruby for a nice long walk. And maybe on the way back we can stop and have an ice cream. Won't that be fun?" In this view, raw experiential material is mediated right from the start by parents' use of storylike language to translate the world for their children.

In Nelson's commentary on the Emily tapes, she emphasizes, to a greater extent than in her previous work, the role of language as a form of mediation that creates order in the world. A focus on language as a system that creates order contrasts with the views that language merely maps or reflects the objective order of the world, or that human beings' perceptions of the world are innately given. In other words, in this alternative conception, language constructs the experience it describes rather than merely reflecting that experience.

Jerome Bruner and Joan Lucariello focus specifically on Emily's use of language to mediate her experience in their analysis of the tapes. They argue that Emily uses her monologues to learn about the narrative form itself, an essential human form for making sense. Although language in general may help us organize experience, narrative language and the narrative thought it shapes play a special role in integrating affect, cognition, and action. Bruner and Lucariello begin with the premise that early in life, action, feelings, and knowledge are undifferentiated. The young child experiences these aspects in a global or holistic way. Once we recast our experience into story form, we gain some distance from it. Narrative gives the child a form for distancing herself, for disentangling feelings, thoughts, and actions. "The means for the child's more reliably distinguishing what she does from what she feels from what she knows or experiences about the world is," Bruner and Lucariello argue, "inherent in the structure of narrative discourse."

What is it about the narrative form that facilitates the ordering and understanding of experience? Bruner and Lucariello suggest five features of narrative that contribute to this process: sequencing, canonicalization, stance taking, intentionalization, and metacommentary.

By reconstructing experiences in a narrative form, children put events into a coherent, meaningful order, a sequence: "We went to Grandma's house and then we ate turkey." Children also use such words as "usually," "once," and "sometimes" to mark the distinction between typical and special events—thus, canonicalization: "And usually Grandpa sings, but *this time* I sang, too." They convey perspective, or stance taking: "We went to Grandma's house" (an experience that includes the story-teller and that happened in the past). In intentionalization, they assign feelings and goals to the characters in their stories: "And Toby wanted to get the wishbone, but I got it and Toby cried. He was mad." And, through metacommentary, they comment on the meaning of the event or on the story itself: "First Grandpa sang, then I sang. It was great!"

These narrative components allow children to create accounts of events they have experienced and, perhaps most importantly, to focus on understanding unusual affect-laden experiences (such as the birth of a sibling) in relation to the compelling structure of everyday routines.

Children listen to and tell stories to gain understanding in two senses, cool and hot, to use Bruner's terms. "Cool" knowledge usually draws on what we call cognition; it refers to how things work in the physical world, what comes first and what follows, how people, things, and actions fit together. Understanding in the "hot" sense refers to understanding feelings and emotional concerns: Why did my parents yell? What kind of person am I? It's scary when the lights go out. What makes my younger brother sad? It draws on feelings as much as cognition.

Problem Solving

◆

Emily often tells stories about events that have some confusing kernel—a cognitive puzzle she needs to work on, as Carol Feldman has pointed out. Emily uses terms of logical inference such as "but," "so," "not," and "because" and terms describing her state of knowledge—"maybe," "probably," "certainly"—on appropriate occasions, most often when she is puzzling through an event whose meaning is unclear to her. For instance, Emily doesn't understand why her father cannot run in a race she is looking forward to:

> Today Daddy went, trying to get into the race but the people said no so he, he has to watch it on television. I don't know why that is, maybe 'cause there's too many people. I think that's why, why he couldn't go in it, . . . So he has to watch it on television, . . . on Halloween day, then he can run a race and I can watch him. I wish I could watch him. But they said non non non. Daddy Daddy Daddy! . . . No no, No no.

The puzzle-solving use of narrative is not only helpful when very young children are first building up a store of event representations and tackling certain basic problems of causality and order. As children get older they may use the narrative form in larger contexts to solve more elaborate cognitive puzzles.

"Sometimes getting in trouble can save your life!" my 7-year-old son announced one day upon arriving home from school. I asked him to tell me more.

Well, I was singing to myself when Mrs. Ladd was giving the reading instructions today, so she said I had to stay inside during recess and do the reading, because I hadn't been listening to the instructions so I was behind. So at recess I stayed inside. But all the other kids, who went outside, got in big big *trouble, and they had to come in and sit down with their heads on their desks, and they weren't allowed to do anything. And I had been so good doing my reading, and since I hadn't been outside when they got in trouble, I got to read for the whole rest of the afternoon while they were punished.*

My son was not only sharing an important experience, he was also sorting out some information about how the world works and trying to develop a logical formula to explain how he could both get in trouble and get the best deal after all. In this way, the cognitive puzzles of the first two years of life are replaced by more abstract and layered puzzles in later life.

While some stories seem to reveal a single problem a child is concerned with, children may also use the same story to puzzle through several different problems at once. Thus 4-year-old Stella uses a narrative form to address a question about social relations and also to get some grip on the relationship between reality and its representation in narrative. Stella, who is white, arrived at school one day and walked over to one of her teachers, Robert, a black man. She told him she had a story she wanted to tell him, but she was afraid it might upset him. He reassured her that it would not upset him, so she began:

"A long time ago, black people weren't allowed on the front of the bus. Does this upset you?" to which he replied, "No, it doesn't upset me. So who was allowed to sit on the front of the bus?" She continued, "Only white people were allowed on the bus." Robert asked, "And then what happened?" Stella answered: "I don't know. I haven't heard the rest of the tape yet."

Stella is clearly puzzled by the differential treatment of whites and blacks. She seems equally drawn to solving the puzzle of how stories relate to real life. She knows that this is relevant enough so that a black person might be upset to hear her account. The most charming and perhaps most intriguing part of the story, however, is that she doesn't know the answer to his question because she has not yet heard the rest of the tape. This suggests that she has a clear sense of what her source of knowledge is (the story on the tape) and a sense of narrative boundaries. Stories have ends, and you don't get all the information until you've heard the whole story.

Making Emotional Sense of the World

If children tell stories as a way of solving cognitive puzzles in their world, they also use stories to make emotional sense of themselves and the people around them. This is the other side of Stella's story. As much as Stella is trying to resolve the cognitive problem of the relation of story representation and real life, she is also using the story to try to come to grips with an issue of emotional concern, why blacks and whites are treated differently. Finally, her initial reluctance to tell the story to a black man whom she likes reveals her dawning awareness of the social and emotional impact of telling stories.

Although for purposes of analysis it is sometimes useful to separate the cognitive and emotional functions of stories, they seldom occur separately. On the contrary, we tackle cognitive problems we care about, and we address emotional problems through cognitive activities, such as rearrangement, distancing through symbolization, and perspective taking.

One of the extraordinary qualities of language is its power to invoke the presence of loved ones even when they are not there. The developmental psychologist and child therapist Jan Drucker has suggested that an infant's dawning awareness of himself as separate from his mother leads to the need for symbolic representations to bridge the newly perceived gap between himself and his parent. Symbols (symbolic gestures, pictures, and, most relevantly, words) connect us to people even as they make us aware of the distance between self and other. In this respect, language functions as a kind of symbolic transitional object, as the child analyst Eleanor Galenson has pointed out.

When the British psychoanalyst D. W. Winnicott first talked about the importance of transitional objects, a concept that he originated, he was speaking about the child's ability to invest some stuffed animal, toy, or blanket with the feelings attached to an important loved one, most often his mother. When the child can hold, look at, and feel the transitional object, the toy or blanket, he receives some of the comfort he would receive from the parent for whom the object is a stand-in.

Winnicott points out that it is the feelings the child projects onto the object that give it this power to represent the parent and to comfort the child. But a child can also invest a repeated dialogue or phrase with the feelings and emotional charge originally directed toward the loved one. The young child can repeat to himself things his mother would say to him if she were there. Or children may tell more elaborate stories about loved ones and past experiences and gain comfort similar to what they find in fondling a teddy bear. This may be partly what Emily is doing when she repeats stories and phrases her parents have used with her.

Emily would often converse with her father just before he left her room at bedtime. He tries to soothe her with his words and give her things to think about that will ease the separation. He encourages her not to cry when he leaves and reminds her of children who don't cry, in contrast to Stephen, her baby brother, who cries because he's just a little baby. After the father leaves one evening, Emily incorporates this conversation into her monologue:

> *Big kids like Emmy and Carl and Linda don't cry. THEY*
> *big kids. THEY sleep like big . . . kids the baby cry at*
> *Tanta's. And the (next over) the next people that came.*
> *Then . . . babies can cry but . . . big kids like Emmy don't*
> *cry . . . they go sleep but the BABIES cry . . . everbod—*
> *the big kids like Emmy don't cry . . . the big kids at*
> *Tanta's cry and (say d-a-h) but the big kids don't cry.*

Emily uses her father's words to help her regulate her own actions. But she may also repeat his words as a way of making him present, as Galenson has suggested.

Narratives are an effective form for making emotional sense of the world partly because of the cooling function they serve. As any analytic patient can attest, talking about something can at the same time revive the experience and evoke the feelings associated with it. But telling about it does not usually create the same intensity of feeling as the original experience. The feeling that some emotional distance has been created may explain why children so enjoy stories about things that they might not like to experience—loss, fear, unrequited love.

One story that young children love to hear is "Are You My Mother?," about a newly hatched bird who cannot find his mother. He spends the whole story searching and searching, asking, "Are you my mother?" of cows, a hen, a truck, and other objects. Such stories fascinate children because they convey some of the feeling, but without the edge or real-life consequences, of the actual experience. Perhaps such early fascination is the precursor to loving books like *Moby-Dick*. As adults, we love to hear and read stories that capture some emotional dilemma but give us enough distance, by virtue of the symbolic form, to experience it without being consumed by it. And, like pretend play, we can experience the feelings without suffering the real-life consequences.

The cooling function of storytelling, and the role it plays in helping to gain mastery over emotions, may also explain children's fascination with repetition. Children are great repeaters. As most parents know only too well, they love to tell the same stories or variations of the same story over and over. They don't, as a rule, do this for the same reason adults do. When adults retell a story, it's usually because the last time it was a great success and they're hoping to achieve the same effect again. Thus, Annie Dillard, in *An American Childhood*, describes her parents' repeated rehearsals of the same joke, each time discussing fine points of emphasis and timing. Children, though, retell stories, or vary them slightly in a succession of repetitions, even when they are alone.

Something other than desire for social success and entertainment is clearly at work. In addition to organizing and understanding their world, kids need to develop some sense of mastery or control over it. They repeat stories in the same way that they practice newly learned games or skills. With each telling they not only can repeat the pleasure or pain of the experience, they repeat the pleasure of telling about the experience, and they gain increased ownership or mastery over both the experience and the telling of it.

"Mommy. Tell it again. Tell about when you fell out of the car when you were a little girl." When children ask for this kind of retelling, they listen with rapt and careful attention, commenting on any change in the way the story is told. For them, listening to a repeated story, especially about an event that has some emotional charge, helps children gain mastery over their feelings and understanding of the experience and mastery over the telling of that experience. It is a way of practicing on two levels, similar to the function served when they retell stories to themselves or an adult.

Along with a sense of vicarious experience, stories allow us to work indirectly on the problems in our own lives, mirrored in the lives of fictional characters. If a young child tells a story about a big mean monster coming through the window, adults are often attuned enough to realize that the storyteller may be scared of big mean monsters. At a deeper level, the listening adult may realize that what gave rise to the storyteller's fear was perhaps a wrathful father, her own erotic or aggressive impulses, a teacher who yelled at her that day, or the troll in "The Three Billy Goats Gruff" that had been read to her earlier that day.

What adults may be less attuned to is the way in which the child uses the story to acquire some sense of comfort and mastery over the potent emotional material. To begin with, the child achieves this sense of mastery simply by telling a story about it. By symbolizing the feelings in a story, she gains possession of it and internalizes it. Once she takes possession of it through the story form, she can change its elements and in that way gain power over it. She might change the story so that the monster is killed by her dog, Bash. Or she might simply retell it again and again, each time changing some detail, like how the monster comes in, who is with her, how the monster acts.

This is a less obvious form of gaining mastery, a less dramatic rearrangement of events. But it shows, nonetheless, the power of the narrative form to name a reality that you can then reshape in imagination. This is similar to what Bruno Bettelheim meant, in *The Uses of Enchantment,* when he spoke of the power of fairy tales to provide children with material with which to think about fundamental and vivid emotional concerns.

It is not just the newly emerging narrator, the toddler like Emily, who uses stories to understand and work through troubling emotions. The classroom teacher and writer Vivian Paley has given us some of the most dramatic examples of somewhat older children resolving their emotional dilemmas through their stories. For instance, in *The Boy Who Would Be a Helicopter,* Paley traces the experiences of one preschooler in her classroom, Jason, as over the course of the school year he emerges from relative social isolation into the world of his peers.

As a teacher, Paley used storytelling as a tool to help Jason out of his isolation. As an observer and writer, she uses his and the other children's stories to understand and demonstrate his social and emotional transformation. In the beginning his exclusive preoccupation with helicopter play manifests his separateness from the other children. Paley's classroom emphasizes collaborative play and storytelling, yet Jason will not allow other children to contribute to his stories or play with him using his helicopter theme. The rigidity of his stories and storytelling process reflects a personal rigidity.

Thus, Paley encourages him to use his helicopter stories to express his ideas, concerns, and interests. At times she uses his story theme herself to communicate ideas and suggestions to him, and encourages the other preschoolers to communicate with Jason through his stories and their own. Over the year, she subtly guides him toward elaborations and modifications of his stories that bring him into greater contact with the other children. Through storytelling he learns to coordinate with the other kids, entering into their play stories and allowing them to participate in his. Through his stories Jason makes himself sympathetic and comprehensible to his peers. His stories are both a tool and a reflection of this emotional transformation.

The telling and retelling of emotionally significant incidents allows children to work through experience in several ways. Each retelling occurs in a context that gives it a new thrust or impact. Each retelling allows for, and communicates, the changing meaning of the story to the person telling it. Retelling allows the child to explore the ever expanding layers of complexity within the story and the storytelling situation. In this next example the child also uses the retelling of an emotionally charged experience to learn about the intricacies of the social world and her place within it.

A 6 year old, Kara, had a fight with her baby-sitter, Andy, which culminated when they came to find Kara's mother in her study. Both were upset, and both turned to Kara's mother for help in sorting it out. While she sobbed and lay on her mother's bed, Kara told a little of what happened.

The story the mother got from this information we can call Narrative 1: Kara and Andy had been blowing out eggshells to decorate for Easter. Kara wanted to cook the raw eggs. Andy said no, because the eggs were dirty and had feathers in them and she thought it unsafe. Kara continued to prepare them for cooking by adding milk. Again, Andy told Kara not to. Kara replied angrily, "Why not?" Andy, irritated, said, "*Now*, it's because I said so," at which point Kara called Andy a jerk, and Andy sent Kara to her room. Kara came out of her room holding a closed jackknife. This is when they came and found Kara's mother.

The two adults stepped outside the room. After telling the mother her version of what had happened (Narrative 2), Andy left. Kara lay on her mother's bed sobbing and said she was the most miserable she had ever been, repeating parts of her original story (Narrative 1). Then they dropped the subject while they got ready to go on an errand in the car.

When they got in the car, Kara said in an angry voice, "So. What did Miss Baby Innocent tell you about what happened?" and the mother told Kara a little of what the baby-sitter had reported to her. Call this Narrative 3, the mother's version, to Kara, of the baby-sitter's story. Mother and daughter discussed it at some length—how Andy must have felt, how Kara felt, and what the incident meant. Kara seemed to feel better, understand the baby-sitter's side of it, and appeared relieved that her mother seemed to understand Kara's side (including her "real intention" with the knife, as opposed to the baby-sitter's interpretation based on Kara's action). The story or stories (Narratives 1, 2, and 3) appeared finished.

A week later, Kara and her mother were sitting around the dinner table with Kara's grandparents. Kara began to tell her grandparents the story of her encounter with Andy. She insisted that she had to "tell the *whole* story, beginning at the beginning." This we might call Narrative 4, Kara's retelling of the story, including her reporting of the subsequent retellings. As she told it, she tried to convey her view of the incident and the parts of it that she still did not accept, such as when Andy had said no to cooking the eggs, "for *no reason.*"

What was most interesting about this final retelling was the emotion it evoked in Kara. Her face began to change color, her eyes filled, and the feelings that had originally been triggered by the incident were triggered once again in the rebuilt narrative. We cannot know how Kara finally felt about the episode or in what way repeating it as a story made her feel better. But it clearly shows how a narrative holds in it, by virtue of its sequence, timing, buildup, character, and complex perspective construction, the power to re-create a scene in a way that mere reference to an event does not.

Kara might have said, "I had a fight with Andy last week," and felt little more than a dim stirring of the feelings the fight had caused. But in telling the story of an experience, a child relives, albeit with a more manageable intensity, the feelings, pleasures, and conflicts that occurred in the first place. This anecdote is also a dramatic instance of the layers a story accumulates as it becomes part of the child's repertoire. Like the game "I packed my grandmother's bag and in it I put . . . ," a story collects meanings as it is retold, and the retellings add depth to the emotional, cognitive, and dramatic action of the original story.

Becoming Part of the Culture

···························· ◆ ····························

In *Ways with Words,* the ethnographer Shirley Brice Heath contrasts the storytelling styles of two small communities in the American South, Roadville and Trackton. Brice Heath spent a total of nine years living in these two communities, participating in and recording the ways in which the families worked, played, and raised their children. She focused specifically on each community's way of talking and using language.

Brice Heath found that the two communities have distinctive purposes for storytelling, value different kinds of stories, and use different means to impart these storytelling values to their children. In Roadville, a white working-class community of textile employees, people tell stories primarily to teach and perpetuate religious and moral values. As Brice Heath characterizes it, Roadville parents teach their children how to tell stories. In Trackton, a neighboring community of black working-class families who are also employed in the mills, people tell stories to entertain each other, gain control over one another in social gatherings, and demonstrate their social desirability to one another. In Trackton, children learn to tell stories through participation in storytelling situations rather than through direct instruction. Part of the task of growing up in either community is learning how to tell the right kind of story for the right kind of purpose.

Language is the child's passport into his culture. If this is true of language in general, it is particularly true of narratives. Narratives, on the one hand, have some universality. As the philosopher Hadyn White points out, one can recognize a story from any culture. On the other hand, each culture, each community, has its own way of telling stories. The British psychologist F. C. Bartlett showed in his experiments on individual and group memory that if you tell a story to one person in a community, and have the person retell it to someone else, and then have that person retell it to a third person, and so on and so on (like the game of telephone), the story undergoes small changes with each retelling, and these changes will reflect subtle cultural differences in ways of seeing and saying things from one group and person to the next.

Bartlett's point was that remembering is a social process, and that in the act of recalling (and retelling) a story, we transform it to fit the way we think, which is shaped by the culture and subculture in which we live. Thus, the way a story is told reflects membership in a cultural community. By telling stories that are engaging and informative in a way that the community deems appropriate, one can more easily and successfully enter into the culture. This is as true for adults as it is for children.

We all know the feeling of being a newcomer to a particular group, be it a school, a workplace, or a social network. Learning what is considered funny, what people want to hear and talk about, what level of detail to include and privacy to respect in your stories is part of becoming a member of the group. And what richer source of information about a group is there than the stories the people around you tell about their experiences.

For the child, the social world as a whole must be entered, for the first time, and mastered. Children listen to the stories told around them to get clues about the culture they are growing up in, and they use this information to try and become increasingly adept at functioning within their community. Sarah Michaels has shown that within a classroom, learning how to tell the "right" kind of story greatly affects the type of feedback a child gets from her teacher. Michaels recorded the stories black and white children told in classrooms run by white teachers. Often the type of story and story response the black children were comfortable with were subtly unacceptable to the white teachers. For instance, a child might tell a story that doesn't contain any apparent moral, in a classroom taught by a teacher who believes all stories should clearly articulate or imply a moral. At the end of her story, the teacher says simply, "Uh, huh. What's the point?" The child doesn't know how to answer this question because she didn't organize her story around a moral. She leaves the interaction feeling either inadequate, stupid, or out of step with the group of which she is supposed to be a member. Stories are a way of learning what is important in your group and a good way of showing that you belong.

Making and Keeping Friends

Two 6 year olds who have known each other a long time are planning a trip to a soda fountain without their parents:

Daniel: C'mon it'll be fun. She said we could have ice cream and milk shakes.

Simone: Mmm. OK. Should I go? Or shouldn't I? I don't know whether I should go or not. It's not that I'm scared to go without a grown-up. I just don't know if I should or not.

Daniel: Yeah. Remember last time you were too scared. You didn't want to be alone with me and Tim. Remember? You thought someone might try and take us. But then you came running up and said you did want to go. And remember? We each got chocolate mint chip. And Tim got the change, and gave us each a nickel. And you were lucky you came because if you hadn't come, you wouldn't have got a nickel.

Simone: Yeah, I was scared that time, and you laughed at me. But this time I'm not scared. OK. I'll come too.

Stories, especially ones about personal experience, are a powerful tool for managing social relations. Through stories, children present themselves to one another. Research has shown that conversations are longer among children who know each other, suggesting that intimacy, shared experience and shared knowledge, leads to higher levels of conversational ability in early childhood. One way in which children develop that intimacy is through the stories they tell each other.

For example, one often hears friends, especially between the ages of 6 and 10, huddling together and going over favorite shared experiences. It is not uncommon for friends who get together only occasionally to warm up to one another through the recounting of favorite shared experiences: "Remember that time when we were out under the tree, and we saw that turkey?" "Yeah, and when we heard that sound we were like ahhhgrr, what's that?" "Yeah, and you climbed up on the rock."

We often think of talking and doing as separate processes, separate activities. But this view neglects to take into account the social force of language. Talking is a kind of doing, and telling stories is a kind of action. The philosopher Paul Ricoeur, in a wonderful essay about the relationship between studying narratives in texts and studying them in dialogues, explores the idea that narratives are a kind of speech act. This builds on the ideas of the philosophers John Searle and J. L. Austin, who first proposed that when we talk we don't merely talk about things, we do things (promise, marry, condemn, convince). Viewed as a kind of speech act, every story has three components: the actual story as it is told, what the speaker intended to achieve with the story, and the effect the story has on the listener. This framework helps us see how people might use stories to interact with and affect others.

Children playing with one another may be particularly prone to using stories as a kind of speech act. For young children, there are a variety of ways to interact, disagree, resolve conflicts, share experience, and have fun. One of the primary ways they do these things is through language. And among the linguistic genres available to them is the narrative. In the dialogue between Daniel and Simone, a child is trying to decide whether to join her friend on an outing. She and her friend draw on a past experience to clarify the present dilemma. This in itself marks a developmental milestone, because at an earlier stage each would simply have kept stating her or his wish or fear or have turned to an adult for help. Now they can turn instead to their versions of a past experience to help them sort out the situation and understand each other's part in it.

In this next example, two 3 year olds use the story mode to entertain one another and to increase their feelings of affiliation. Hanna and Emily are sitting at a table drawing pictures:

Hanna says, "Once the candy man came to my house and he brought me lots of candy. And he brought me chocolate. And he brought me a sugar Easter egg." Emily, who has been watching and listening to Hanna with a delighted look on her face, breaks in: "Yes. Once the candy man came to *my* house, and he brought me *lots* and *lots* of candy, and he was wearing no underpants." Both girls erupt into laughter, and then Hanna picks up the story: "The candy man came to *my* house, and his *bottom* showed, and he had no pants on." The girls giggle delightedly and continue with their drawing.

A narrative structure also allows children to guide one another through play, as Wells has pointed out. For instance, if a group of children are building a structure in the block corner, the articulation of a narrative theme or basic plot helps them assign roles and agree on rules of what can happen within the pretend scenario. If they are making a house, and one of them is the mother, and two are workers, and another is the father, this outlines the procedures ("you have to bring in the wood, because you're the builder") and generates play sequences ("and then let's say that it was raining, and we all had to duck inside our house, and the mommy and daddy said they would make dinner for the workers").

Preschool children can devote a great deal of energy and ability to collaborative storytelling with their friends. A student and I looked at the ways in which children establish and maintain feelings of intimacy through storytelling. We found that 4 and 5 year olds can become involved in highly coordinated storytelling. In many of these narratives, children took on well-defined authorial tasks and coordinated their chosen roles so that a good play story could emerge. For instance, two little girls playing with some farm toys began to develop their play through a story involving several dramatic themes: storms, parental abandonment, and illness. But most striking was how clear and interdependent their roles were within this narrative framework. One little girl, Mimi, was responsible for setting the scene and describing action, while her friend, Sharon, consistently chimed in at the right moments:

Mimi: Now the storm is over and . . .
Sharon: Oh, well.
Mimi: The storm is not ever coming again. *(Gasps)* A rainbow, a rainbow, a rainbow!

Sharon: (in a baby voice) Yippee! Mama, Mama, MAma, MAma.

Mimi: Pretend the children were going up to the top and they were not supposed to *(puts dolls on roof)*. Pretend the children were gonna get hurt at the end.

Sharon: (in high voice, holding mother doll) See, I told you guys that you would get hurt if you climbed up here. Now get in your rooms and have a time-out!

These examples show how children use storytelling as a way of guiding play and other social interactions. But creating stories is also a form of play in its own right and becomes an increasingly important one between the ages of 4 and 7.

As with other forms of symbolic play, the medium itself gives rise to certain delights and discoveries, interesting problems that may intrigue the child as much as the "thing" she is trying to express. Just as a child who is painting may become so absorbed in the dripping paint, the texture, the color, the look of the brush going on the page, that she will momentarily, or permanently, forget about the scene she had planned to depict, so, too, the young storyteller may become so intrigued with the sounds of the words she is using, the excitement of some particular narrative device, that the original content, or point of the story, becomes lost.

Steven is sitting in the back of the car on the way home from day care. He has been showing his mother, who is driving, that he has snuck home a toy that belonged to Charlie, a playmate:

Tomorrow, I am going to pull this toy out of my pocket and Charlie is going to say, "Hey, that's mine," and I am going to say, "No, I brought this from home." [Steven changes his voice to indicate another speaker.] *"Oh, but*

that looks just like mine." [He changes voices again.]
"Yeah? Well, it's not, it's mine." And then I'm gonna say,
"Hey, wanna see this green monster [holding up the toy]?
He can fly [makes blowing and whirring noises], *and then
the monster goes swishsssss, and then he goes whrrrrrr,
and then he goes down like this."*

This monologue began as a story about a possible conflict
over a toy and an act of deception that one child is imagining
he will perpetrate on another. But the pleasures of a story
about the sounds and motions of the toy itself overtake the
original purpose of the story and transform it into a game of
sound making.

Children use stories to understand their world, or to take
an extreme constructivist position, to invent their world. But
when they tell stories as a way of playing, they are also using
narratives as a way to re-invent their world. Storytelling
is, after all, at heart a creative act. As with other creative and
symbolic media, the author has a unique power to manipulate
characters and scenes to make the world appear as he wishes
or dreads it to be, or both. And, as with other symbolic media,
the language is opaque rather than transparent. The words, the
sentences, and the sounds are interesting and noticeable
beyond the message, or content, they convey. In everyday
practical conversation, we look through the words to the
message, thus rendering the words transparent. With many
children's stories, just as in good poetry, words and phrases
are as interesting and important as the meaning they convey,
thus rendering them opaque. We can still see through to the
meaning, but the shade and nuance of the language affect our
understanding of the meaning.

Suppose a child of 5 is playing with cowboy and Indian
figures. At first this is primarily an enactive type of play, in

which the symbolizing consists of conferring real life and action on the little figures. At times the little boy narrates his activity ("Now the Indian is going to jump on his horse."), and then he switches into dialogue in which he is providing the voices for the characters ("Ahghhh, ya got me. I'm gonna shoot yer friend for that."). Now suppose he turns to his mother and says: "The cowboy, he jumps, he swings, he slips, he dies. He was one of the bad guys. The Indian, he jumps, he swings, he rides—he was one of the good guys." What began as a kind of narration, integral to and part of the play activity, now takes off and becomes a form of play in and of itself, in which the content is blended with the sounds of the words, the rhythm of the sentences. Stories, then, can guide and clarify play, but they can also be a form of play, one that can be used by the solitary player as well as the narrator(s) in a collaborative setting, where the storytelling itself may be collaborative.

Constructing a Self

It has been said that everyone, in telling the story of his own life, casts himself as either the conquering or the suffering hero. This self-concept, cast in literary terms, may begin early in life, through the types of stories and the tone of the stories young children tell about themselves. Even young children depict themselves as some kind of hero.

Children tell stories to organize their experience and their knowledge and to communicate that knowledge to others. When Kara told and retold the story about herself and her baby-sitter, she was working through an upsetting experience and trying to share some of her experience with her relatives.

But stories not only reconstruct experience and communicate experience, they are experience. And through the stories we tell, especially the stories we tell about ourselves, we construct ourselves. As discussed more fully in Chapter 7, if you listen to 2 year olds talking about their past, it is easy to imagine that by telling about something, they make that experience part of their self-concept: I am the person who bought a red lollipop and shared it with my grandpa. I am the person who took a bubble bath and made a beard out of bubbles. I am the person who rode my bicycle all the way down the driveway, and my mother was worried about me.

The cognitive psychologist Ulric Neisser says that one of the ways we know ourselves is through the construction of an extended self. It is the self we imagine, picture, and dwell on from the past and into the future. At any given moment how we behave, feel, and experience ourselves grows, in part, out of the self we have woven together from all our past experiences and imaginings about the future.

A friend was driving in a car with her 6 year old, and his pants got wet with juice. She took his pants off, and rolled up a jacket for a pillow and put his father's jacket over him as a blanket so that he could sleep for the rest of the long drive. Suddenly he piped up, "I have a jacket for a pillow, and a jacket for a blanket, and no pants on. I feel like a homeless person." We project ourselves into different possible experiences as a way of exploring who we are and who we are not. Clearly, part of who we are is shaped by the people we imagine being. This is related, in turn, to the benefits of literacy later in life. Works of imaginative literature enrich us partly because they allow us to enter into the lives and experiences of others. When we temporarily merge with a character in a novel or short story, we add dimension to our personal identity. When children tell stories about who they might be, wish they were, imagine being, they are trying on one of the other selves that are part of the entire self we each ultimately are.

Inventing and Adapting

◆

As children build up a more or less solid set of guiding principles and representations of experience (as they, for example, build up a repertoire of scripts and begin to develop some flexibility of operation within those scripts), they do what is perhaps most singular and wonderful about being human: They change things around. The splendid thing about a symbol system is that it can be used to describe or encode reality in a way that is socially consensual, reliable enough so that the description fits experience across people and over time. This is the sense in which the scripts, and the mental representations from which they are derived, are veridical and based on reality. They give us the feeling that we live in a world that is stable, shared, apprehensible, and relatively predictable.

The best thing about symbolizing your world is that you can also alter things about the world in your imagination and in the world itself. It's comforting and adaptive for everyone to agree that the sky is blue, but it is exciting and enriching to suggest that the sky is silver, or that it is lonely, or that it cries. By the same token, it is useful for the child to be able to tell his mother that he played with blocks at school, and that he ate macaroni and cheese for lunch. It is adaptive, for other reasons, for a child to be able to say that during schooltime she traveled to the moon, and that the teacher served cotton candy for lunch.

Children tell stories not only to represent experience as they know it to be, as they know others know it to be, but they also tell stories to represent experience as they would like it to be. This is not simply a way of expressing deep-seated wishes or fantasies. The act of remaking your world serves a function in and of itself, beyond the expression of any unconscious wishes. The imaginative control you gain over the world by being able to decide, at least symbolically, who does what to whom and what things look and sound like is itself a vital component of human experience. This is what play researchers are referring to when they talk about the value of imaginary play: The child gets to have things just as she wishes.

Children use narratives to achieve a whole host of important tasks in the process of development. Like language in general, narratives have the power to be about something, at the same time that they do something. A narrative refers to, conveys, describes, and represents experiences people have. A story can be about a trip to the beach, a fight between neighbors, or a first airplane ride, but stories always *do* something as well. They entertain, teach, convince, evoke, control, explain, justify, clarify. Stories are both a product of a developmental process and a vehicle through which development takes place.

3

◆

Perspectives on Narrative

◆

Whether I shall turn out to be the hero of my own life, or whether that station will be held by anybody else, these pages must show. To begin my life with the beginning of my life, I record that I was born (as I have been informed and believe) on a Friday, at twelve o'clock at night. It was remarked that the clock began to strike and I began to cry simultaneously.

George found a girlfriend in the mall. Her name was Sara. They liked each other because they were both plain.

So begin two very different stories. And yet both *are* stories. The first is the opening to *David Copperfield,* the second the opening to a story told by a 7 year old. Despite their differences, these two stories have much in common. Both were constructed for an audience, and both were conceived by their authors as imaginative works, as constructions of an alternate reality. A story, whether told by a child or by an adult, creates a world that may or may not be based on the real events experienced or known by the author.

Dickens's *David Copperfield* begins at the beginning—the beginning, that is, of a person's life. The implicit suggestion is that the beginning of a story matches the beginning of some definable real-life event—birth, in this case. He tells us right away that every story not only has a beginning, but a hero. It also has an author who can speculate about the events he describes. He tells his reader that he has a twofold relationship to his story—he constructed it, but it has a life of its own that may surprise even him. He sets up for us the triad of author, text, and audience that is implicit in every narrative.

The 7 year old's story also begins with a hero, or two. But it has no prelude. It alludes to no theory of storytelling, no framing of the act of writing or reading a narrative; it gives no warning that you are about to read a story. It begins at the beginning not of any clearly defined life event but of an imagined relationship. It assumes, as most stories by 7 year olds do, and some stories by adult writers, that the reader has accepted a silent invitation to enter a fictive world.

We study the writings of authors like Dickens or Tolstoy because they are great works of art. The reasons for studying the stories children tell are rather different but can be just as compelling. Children's stories reveal the development of literacy and narrative ability and can tell us a great deal about what is going on in the emotional and intellectual life of the individual child.

Wallace Chafe, who analyzed the stories people of different cultures told in response to seeing *The Pear Stories,* a short silent movie he made, put this nicely: "I see narratives as overt manifestations of the mind in action: as windows to both the content of the mind and its ongoing operations." Although the reasons for studying children's stories can be quite different from those for analyzing great novels, many of the same issues of author's intention, voice, relation of content to narrative form, and effect on the audience that preoccupy literary critics also arise in investigating children's stories.

Studying Narrative

◆

There are a multitude of things to look at, or look for, in children's stories. Developmental psychologists and linguists such as Wallace Chafe, Nancy Stein, and Allyssa McCabe have looked at the structure of children's stories as a way of conceptualizing the structure of the child's thinking. How is the story put together? Does it have a beginning, a middle, and an end? Are the sentences related to one another in a logical way? How many episodes are in the story, and what connects them? How many words are used to embellish the central event or action?

Clinical psychologists, on the other hand, are more interested in what the stories are about and what this reveals about the teller's emotional life. What conflicts are evident in the action? Does the teller portray himself as the protagonist? How are other family members described? What does the storyteller reveal about earlier events in his life?

A few investigators study the process of storytelling itself. What motivates the person to want to tell a story? Does she revise her story in response to different audiences? What is the interaction between conversational partners in the construction of a story?

Although these approaches are not mutually exclusive, most researchers concentrate on only one aspect or another. The strength of such single-mindedness is clarity. Choosing one aspect of storytelling—process, content, or structure—allows you to be more precise. The danger is that the analysis may end up giving the impression (to investigator and reader alike) that form can somehow exist separately from content, or that the process of constructing a story is not integrally related to its form.

Meaning in Children's Stories

◆

Children share with great authors a kind of vital connection between the content of their story and its form. They have something they urgently want to convey, and they have to find or invent a form to express it. In everyday adult life many of us use fairly routine forms to tell what has happened to us. Rarely do we make up stories for or with one another. And we are unlikely to explore different ways of telling a story when we do. But for a young child, just as for a great adult author, what she wants to relate helps to determine how she says it.

> What do young children care about? First and foremost, themselves. Their earliest needs are associated with realizing themselves, becoming aware of their own names, feeling the psychological position in the family. These needs constitute the matrix of their earliest interests. Their first comprehensions are deeply personal: who they are, what they do, what they have, how they get it, where they live, where they go, what they like, what they don't like, what frightens them, what thrills them.

These comments from Barbara Biber, educator and one of the founders of the innovative Bank Street College of Education, are also an apt description of the typical content of young children's stories. Young children's stories are likely, in some way or another, to be about the self and to be filled with information about their families, what they do, what they have, where they live, what has happened to them, what frightens and what thrills them. For creative adults and the youngest storytellers, the urge to convey such personal experience is the force that drives the discovery of narrative form. Sometimes that urge is dominated by the content of the experience, as in a 5 year old's conversation with his father:

"Ya know what? Yesterday, when me and Jason and Ryder were over at Grandma's pond? Well, instead of finding frogs we found bones with brown stuff on it."
"Yeah?"
"And we thought it was a deer or a wolf. And it had teeth. On the bones. Over near the stump where there's this skinny tree in it."

In this case the structure is simple: A highlighted event is placed in the context of ongoing action. The framework or plot of the story is implicit: kids looking for frogs. The urgency, however, comes from the excitement of what the story is about: bones were discovered. With young children the excitement or saliency of the content makes it imperative to share with just about anybody. This is the reason why a sympathetic visitor to a day-care center may be regaled with personal anecdotes.

At other times the desire to connect with the audience takes precedence over the content. For instance, when two children are playing and one tells a story that is particularly funny or exciting, the friend may be so eager to join in the pleasures of swapping stories that he may make up one on the spot, or retell a version of the story he has just heard. He doesn't have much to tell, but he sure wants to tell it.

For adult authors and young children, there are two tension points, the urge to express a particular content and the urge to communicate with a particular audience—along which every story is strung. Where the teller's interest or motivation falls at any given moment helps to determine what kind of story he or she will tell.

In the late 1970s and early 1980s the emphasis in research on children's narrative was on cognitive processes and computer models of thinking. Although it is useful to conceptualize some human activity in terms of paths with alternatives, decision trees, and flowcharts, this emphasis causes us to lose sight of the importance of meaning in human mental functioning. Unlike a computer, we are always seeking and creating meaning. And meaning is what is most important about narratives. The author's meaning is what drives a story, determines the shape it takes, and gives the listener the impulse to understand the story.

A mother in an elementary school is telling me about her son Sacha, who is 6. Sacha is confused about his gender. Since he was 2 years old he has played only with girls, chosen stereotypically girl toys and clothing, and said he wished he were a girl. He has been in therapy for the past year. He seems a lot better in his mother's view, as he no longer constantly expresses the wish to be a girl. But she's still worried. When he has play dates with girls, he talks about them in "living color," recounting their visits in rich detail. "We played this and then Ruby did this and this, and you know she said this, and at Ruby's house. . . ." But on the rare occasions when he agrees to a play date with Ben, the one boy he likes, his stories are very different. "It's as if he experiences the boys in black and white," Sacha's mother says. When she asks how his play date with Ben was, he looks distant and says "fine" or "okay," and if she asks what they did, he'll answer in a monotone, "played."

In this case the form of Sacha's responses tells us something about his meaning. The stories about girls are elaborate, filled with detail, and told with feeling. His answers about boys are spare and often do not even constitute real stories. The form and the content are perfectly integrated to reveal the meaning.

Recent studies of children's narratives have begun to explore how the personal meaning of remembered events affects children's recall of those events. Judy Hudson, for example, has shown that emotion plays a significant role in determining what aspects of an event are described. She and her colleagues found that when preschoolers tell about a happy experience they focus on re-creating the happy moment and are less likely to tell the story in a dynamic, action-oriented way. Stories about anger and fear, on the other hand, are more likely to resemble conventional stories in that they contain a high point, or conflict, in the middle of the story. In another study, Christine Todd arranged for preschool children to participate in high- and low-emotion events and then tested their narrative recall of those events. The children recalled high-emotion events more vividly and more frequently than low-emotion events. These studies suggest that what someone feels about an event can determine how well it is remembered. It is also possible that the emotional intensity of an experience influences the way the memory is represented and/or communicated to others. In other words, when we try to analyze or characterize any given child's story we can only understand its structure in light of what we think the child might have been feeling, thinking, and doing at the time.

Identifying Narratives

◆

If the structure of a child's story may vary as a function of its meaning, how do we know which things a child says constitute a story and which do not? Every utterance is not necessarily a narrative. We weaken the power of narrative and the power of studying narrative to assume that everything is one, as psychologists Robert Russel and Joan Lucariello wisely point out. Children don't learn about every aspect of themselves and the world through stories. Nor is every conversation or every utterance part of a narrative. On the other hand, narratives are not confined to the ten-minute story hour during day care, nor do Tolstoy and Dickens have a monopoly on the narrative form. Does the speaker need to be aware that she is constructing a narrative? Is it in the ear of the beholder or the lens of the analyst? Should we have different criteria depending on the age of the speaker or writer?

In recent years, numerous criteria have been proposed to delineate narratives from other types of discourse. Among these, several theories seem to offer the most illuminating guidelines for identifying narrative elements in young children's talk and for understanding the different ways in which young children's stories create and evoke meaning. These theories also allow us to think about the ways in which children's stories are similar to and different from the stories adults typically tell.

When children tell and write stories, it is harder than it might be with adult stories to make clear decisions about the difference between stories that accurately describe a sequence of experienced events and the more elusive, sometimes more evocative and idiosyncratic utterances that might better be termed narrative fragments, on the one hand, or poetry, on the other. Consider, for instance, two accounts of a Fourth of July party, the first told by a 6 year old, the second by her 7-year-old cousin:

> *I loved that beach party. Remember? Those boom, bazoom, Christmas tree, orange and green, bazeen pow lights.*

> *This year was the best Fourth of July party we ever went to. It was right on the beach, and the fireworks looked so close up and so big.*

While both children recall the experience, the first imparts little objective information about what actually happened, instead offering a highly personal description, using language unconventionally, to convey what the party evoked in her. Her cousin also gives some emotional flavor to his account but describes it in a way that is both more modulated emotionally and also gives a clearer picture of what happened. We learn less about him and more about the event.

Because narratives are essentially a form of language, it is useful to situate models of narrative in the broader spectrum of discourse. James Britton, who has studied children's language and writing development, and Arthur Applebee, an investigator of children's storytelling, both suggest that there are two types of linguistic interaction, the transactional and the spectator. The transactional consists of logical, "scientific" discussions in which a set of rules governs what is referred to and how it is talked about. Discussions about science, math, and events that have actually happened, or about specific problems in the workplace all typically occur in transactional language. This type of discourse is called transactional because one participant can understand, evaluate, and respond to what the other participant says as the narrative progresses. The listener and speaker can work through a problem or a topic together, and each statement in turn can be interpreted by itself, according to the rules or conventions governing discussion on the topic. Suppose someone said, "Human beings descended from apes. Apes evolved over millions of years, and the species we call *Homo sapiens* evolved from one type of ape." You could stop the speaker at any point and counter what she had said, add something informative to it, or ask for an explanation that would clarify the body of knowledge to which she was referring.

The alternative to transactional language is, according to Britton and Applebee, spectator language, the language of poetry. In hearing or reading, the listener cannot easily participate or interject appropriate information along the way. Instead, the listener must act as the audience or spectator. Each utterance or sentence told in poetic language is dependent on the surrounding sentences or utterances for its meaning and thus cannot be properly evaluated or responded to independently, but only in the context of the whole. What is expressed in spectator language communicates internal, often private, experience or states of feelings. Therefore, two or more people cannot typically collaborate in putting an idea or feeling into words and sentences.

This distinction between transactional and spectator language parallels philosopher Suzanne Langer's contrast between pure logic and pure poetry. Pure logic has set rules that make it available to a group to negotiate, break up, or re-appropriate. Pure poetry, by contrast, is private and shifting and cannot be lifted or separated from the context in which it emerged (the ideas or experiences of the author).

The frameworks of Britton, Applebee, and Langer have many points of overlap with an influential distinction, made by Jerome Bruner, between two models of apprehending the world, the paradigmatic and the narrative. Bruner suggests that we experience and learn about the physical world in a paradigmatic mode (by using arbitrary symbol systems such as algebra and models such as evolution), whereas we understand the cultural world in a narrative mode (through stories, for instance).

The contrasts Britton, Applebee, Langer, and Bruner have proposed are not identical, and each implies somewhat different points about language and people using language. But they all make a distinction between a rule-bound and ultimately arbitrary way of using language and a more dynamic personal way. They all suggest two basic ways of talking about the world and two ways of interacting with other people in talking about the world. Bruner's distinction emphasizes the difference in the subject matter, whereas Applebee and Britton emphasize how participants relate to the text and to one another depending on which kind of language they use. Which kind of language does storytelling involve? The answer is not as simple as it may first appear.

Often narrative language is neither purely transactional nor purely spectator. It can seldom be described accurately as pure poetry or pure logic. In an interview about his work, Jean-Paul Sartre commented that when he wrote philosophy every sentence had one meaning, but that in fiction every sentence had many meanings, many levels of meaning. But this distinction becomes especially blurred when it comes to the sharing of personal experience through storytelling. As we shall see, such stories are often collaboratively told. Even recounting a memory can involve a shared transactional process just as much as a math problem or the description of an experiment might. On the other hand, many children describe events in language that seems more like poetry than descriptive prose. Take, for example, the one cousin's account of the Fourth of July party. When these descriptions are evaluated against adult models of narrative, they are often deemed inadequate or at least immature because they are not transactional in the way that those produced by adults might be.

Perhaps children's stories are impure poems or corrupt scientific accounts. Perhaps Bruner is right when he says that narrative is as much determined by what it is we are trying to talk about as it is by the structure of the product itself. One approach to identifying narratives in the flow of young children's talk is to look simply for language that describes experiences. Using a simple guide like this, one would need to keep in mind that any given description or set of utterances may require a transactional or spectator response. The content of the utterances or, alternately, the stance of the speaker may determine which of the two types of language is used. In more general terms, the distinctions suggested by Applebee, Britton, Langer, and Bruner expand the boundaries of what we call a narrative and allow us to include several types of children's talk and writing in our consideration of the development of narrative processes.

The distinctions I have been describing so far are concerned with the relationship between speaker and listener and suggest that narratives can be participatory or performative (that is, transactional or spectator). But what elements or features should any given piece of text (a child's written work or set of utterances) include to be considered a narrative? Should we base our criteria on a literary model? Must children's narratives contain the same narrative elements as those of accomplished authors or the average adult speaker?

Jerome Bruner has proposed some precise criteria for determining what a narrative is. In his view, a linguistic utterance or set of utterances must contain the following characteristics to qualify as a narrative:

> A narrative must have sequence.

> A narrative must have a plot, a sequence that conveys a meaning.

> A narrative must have a high point, a tension that meets some kind of resolution.

> A narrative remains a narrative whether it is true or untrue. It is "indifferent" to facts.

A narrative makes distinctions between the usual and the unusual (what Bruner terms canonicality and its violations).

A narrative directs attention to personal or subjective experience.

One of the points implicit in these criteria is that through narratives children and adults apprehend the world in highly formal and ritualized ways. The conventions that guide narrative construction and interpretation inform the young storyteller and her listeners about how the world should be experienced, much as the scripts described in Chapter 2 help guide our experiences. These criteria imply that we use stories to formalize our experience and that our stories represent well-shaped cognitions, which, in turn, reflect our culture.

Some children's stories fit Bruner's criteria well, such as this story told by a 5-year-old boy to his mother:

Once there was a monster that lived where other monsters lived just like him. He was nice. He made bad people good. He lived always happy. He loved to play with kids. One day he gets caught in a hurricane. The lights went off except there was flashlights there. He jumped into the ocean. He meeted all the fish. And he lived in the water.

This story establishes a regular setting and set of conditions: a group of monsters who live together happily. The author then introduces canonical tension: something out of the ordinary happens—a hurricane. The events are sequenced. There is the usual state of affairs, and then "one day" a hurricane strikes, and a series of actions follow it. He jumps into the ocean, meets fish, and ends up living in the water. The story has a sense of human (or monster) agency. The monster does things and has subjective experience (lives always happy).

But some children's accounts don't fulfill Bruner's criteria, yet are worth considering as narratives if only because they provide insight into the development of abilities that will later yield full-blown adultlike stories. For instance, among 3 and 4 year olds in a day-care center, many stories are told only partially, either because they are interrupted or because telling a well-formed story is less important to the children than fulfilling the function for which the story is being told. For instance, in this example, two children begin sharing the re-creation of an incident from the day before:

> *Wasn't that funny, Harry, yesterday when Lizzie slipped in the mud? Hahahahaha. She had mud all over her pants and she looked like she pooped in her pants. Hahahaha. And she really looked like a poopy head. Hahahaha. And she looked like a poop on the face. She looked like a shcmoop on the face. Hahahaha.*

This begins as a story. It has some semblance of sequence, and it has a sense of agency, a person who does things (Lizzie slips in the mud). It certainly describes an event that violates the usual and therefore provides dramatic tension. On the other hand, the story is not clearly sequenced, either along logical or temporal lines. There is no high point, no explicit reference to the perspective of the storyteller, and no conclusion or resolution of events, instead ending with a play on words. It contains narrative elements but is incomplete as a story. It nonetheless conveys an experience (albeit elliptically described) occurring in space and time, and it suggests the author's view of the event, a meaning to the story. It has a narrative voice.

Elsewhere, Bruner stresses that sequence must be coupled with meaning in such a way that the sequence serves to create or evoke a particular construal of events, a meaning. When looking at the narratives of adults, for instance, we might not count something as a story if it is merely a sequence, a chronology with no apparent meaning. A curriculum vitae does not count as an autobiographical narrative even though it depicts information in sequence. A person's engagement book does not read as a narrative. There are three reasons for this. For one thing, no language in the engagement book conveys that the notations there refer to a series of things that happened to a particular person, in the past. Nor does the context in which the described events are presented help us detect a meaning. Second, they are not edited for meaning. A sequence of events must be chosen out of the flow of everyday life, and even rearranged if necessary, to convey the meaning, the reason for representing the events. Finally, the adult's engagement calendar lacks any clues to the author-audience relationship; it is not written with others in mind.

On the other hand, if a young child were to walk up to you and say, "I ate my Rice Krispies and then I put on my high tops and then I got in my Dad's truck and then I went to school," that would count as a story, at least the germ of one, because it puts experience into a sequential form. It conveys a sense of agency (someone did something), and through selection it conveys meaning—it lets us know what was important or meaningful to that child. Finally, there is a clear construction of the speaker-listener relationship. Yet, by the time the author is an adult, we will demand that the story be more elaborate, that the meaning of the story be more explicit, and that the conventions earmarking it as a story be more identifiable.

Young children create the world through the selection of what they tell. But they may do it more simply, more incompletely, more opaquely and idiosyncratically than what we expect from adults. Many of the characteristics of narrative are nonetheless contained in their stories and partial stories. The formal criteria of theorists like Bruner are useful as a way of thinking about full-fledged narratives, but they're too narrow if we're going to see the range of children's stories in germ and encourage their development. For parents, the situation is often analogous to that of recognizing a child's first words. Just as parents are quick to notice their child's first attempt at saying a word, they may, if so inclined, be particularly adept at tuning in to their child's early attempts at storytelling and offerings of partial or incomplete stories, even if they are not able to enunciate a set of formal criteria for what constitutes a story. Although linguists and psychologists may rightfully argue that what a parent hears may in part be wishful thinking, the parent has an intuitive grasp of what a word is. More generally, it is essential even for the scientific researcher to maintain a balance between applying fine-grained and clearly defined criteria when identifying narratives and using measures that allow for the simple and natural intuition that "that is a story I just heard" or "there is a story contained in that conversation."

Listening to Children's Stories

All of the approaches we have described take the person's writing or speech as text to be analyzed, with the aid of some framework or set of categories. The analyst acts as a reader, listener, or partner, albeit one using a more explicit set of interpretive rules than a general audience would. The work of J. L. Austin, most notably *How to Do Things with Words* (discussed in Chapter 2), offers a quite different way of analyzing and thinking about narratives. Austin's idea that language could be conceptualized as a series of acts that do things (for example, we marry, we promise, we accuse, we reprimand) spawned a new way of analyzing and describing language behavior, called speech act theory. The unit of analysis became the speech act (utterance or set of utterances) that did something, rather than the traditional unit of words or sentences that referred to something.

A story, like language in general, describes the world. But it also does things. People use stories to convince, impress, inform, and deceive. We can ask, then, of any story or part of a story: How does it affect the listener? What did the listener hear?

According to speech act theory, every utterance has three parts: the locution (what is said), the illocution (what is meant), and the perlocution (the effect of what is said). When narratives are treated as texts, we assume that they have stable meanings or characteristics that we can identify, using some analytic system. We use what is said, the locution, to try to uncover what the storyteller meant or thought or felt, the illocution. But we can also look at the perlocution, the effect of the story on the listener, for a different kind of reading of the text.

Looking at stories through their effects on the audience has both strengths and limitations. Take limitations first: A portrayal of just about anything can have a variety of effects on a person, depending on the individual characteristics of the listener. For instance, a painting of red balloons might make a person feel nostalgic. But that doesn't mean that the painter meant anything nostalgic by it. A list of names rattled off by a child could evoke a narrative in her mother. But that doesn't mean that the child had a story in mind. On the other hand, the strength of focusing on the perlocution, the effect on the reader, is that you are not constantly trying to penetrate the mind of the storyteller. And because stories may have many levels of meaning, you don't have to guess which one the author consciously intended.

If you take a series of utterances that are told as a story, and you take the analytic stance of trying to identify the story that others hear, you give a lot more latitude and credit to the role of the listener or reader in creating meaning. Because all narratives have an audience (at some level or another), and are only real through being heard or read, a listener-oriented approach helps to capture the dynamic by which stories are understood in everyday interactions.

Analyzing stories in terms of what they evoke or mean to a listener is not as outlandish as it may seem. While most conventional psychological research does not depend on something as subjective as a listener's interpretation, current work that focuses on the interpersonal nature of much of our cognitive activity attempts to incorporate this interactive approach to analysis. As Barbara Rogoff has shown in her research on young children's cognitive development, for example, how and what a child thinks while doing a particular learning task depends on how that child has constructed the meaning of the activity. This construction is shaped in part by the way adult and child construe the task through their talk. When people do or say things, the effect of those words or actions on others is at least as meaningful as what those words mean according to a dictionary.

The perlocution approach has a further value. It can, in some instances, help the analyst sidestep the endless regress or arbitrary limitations of a precise literary definition of what a narrative is. The trouble with most criteria for identifying a narrative is that they exclude rich examples of stories and storylike utterances. For instance, if a story must have a dramatic climax, many children's descriptions of events would be excluded that otherwise are rich in their depiction of past experiences. If one insists that a story must put actions and events into a temporal framework and locate events in a space, many fine pieces of adult literature would be excluded as well.

Consider, for example, this excerpt from Jamaica Kincaid's *Girl*, a piece that is only a few pages long and is made up solely of things that a mother and daughter say to each other, without any indication or instruction to the reader that this is so.

Wash the white clothes on Monday and put them on the stone heap; wash the color clothes on Tuesday and put them on the clothesline to dry; don't walk barehead in the hot sun; cook pumpkin fritters in very hot sweet oil; soak your little cloths right after you take them off; when buying cotton to make yourself a nice blouse, be sure that it doesn't have gum on it, because that way it won't hold up well after a wash; soak salt fish over-night before you cook it; is it true that you sing benna in Sunday school?

The reader knows not only that this conveys an experience and an event of sorts but also what the story is about. Even though it does not contain the usual characteristics of a narrative, we know that some necessary narrative elements are at work because of the experience they create in the reader.

The literary critic Tsevetan Todorov has added a further twist to the different perspectives on narrative, as seen in his diagram of the relationship among text, author, and reader:

1. The author's narrative   4. The reader's narrative
            ↓   ↑
2. Imaginary universe   →   3. Imaginary universe
   evoked by the author   constructed by reader

The compelling aspect of the underlying conceptualization of this diagram is that it allows us to understand any given child's story in terms of what we think the child intended to say, what he actually put into his text, and what meanings his story evoked in a listener. By seeing the child's construction through Todorov's four-part lens, we can look at the different levels of meaning in a story and consider how they are related to one another. It may be, for example, that the relationship between these levels shifts over the course of the child's narrative development.

Thus, when the first cousin told of her Fourth of July experience, No. 1, the author's narrative was spare, consisting of one static event and hinging on a description of one aspect of the event, the lights. But the analyst can attempt to reconstruct No. 2, the imaginary universe of the author, an evening filled with color and excitement, an experience that inspired her to try out a whole new set of words. One can also look at the account in terms of No. 4, the narrative the reader hears, and finally analyze what the little girl said in terms of the world it evokes in the listener, No. 3. Moreover, many children, as they get older, offer a narrative that seems to correspond more closely to the world it evokes in the mind of the listener.

Todorov's formulation allows us to actually apply the idea of shared or intersecting meanings to specific stories. The reader or listener understands some version of the teller's story (and that understanding may or may not match the story the teller intended). In addition, the reader's imaginary universe, the set of meanings, feelings, and ideas which that understood narrative evokes may be similar to or different from the universe of meanings, ideas, and feelings that the author intended to evoke.

In this story told by a 6-year-old girl, there are several ways of approaching the narrative and several potential layers of meaning offered to us:

The Hot Dog

Once upon a time there was a hot dog. And that hot dog was a funny kind 'cause it could talk. And there were only two people who were friends with that hot dog. And their names were Tess and Ella. And they loved it 'cause they thought it was a hot dog! *And they just loved it to pieces. And they were best friends. And they loved and loved each other. And one day they wanted to get married. And both the two girls were fighting over which one would want to be married to the hot dog.*

And so they both got married to the hot dog. And they had such a great time with the hot dog. This hot dog wasn't like something you eat. It was a real dog, but it was always hot. Like a barking dog that was hot. Like fire. Not that hot. Like sweaty. And since they were married they loved playing with each other. But they were only about 6 years old or 7. But no one knows except the two little girls and the hot dog.

One day someone came along walking down the street. And the two little girls and the hot dog saw the person walking down the street. And they said: "We have a hot dog!" And they said: "We want it to be a cold dog!" And that's how Ella and Tess made a cold dog. The End

We can try and figure out what Ella meant by her story and also what feelings and responses the story evoked in her. What is the scene and scenario she imagines and refers to? Her sense of her literal story, and the set of meanings evoked by that sequence may or may not be the same thing. We can also try and identify the universe her story evokes in the reader. What meanings and descriptions does the sequence elicit in us that may or may not be in the mind of the young narrator? Is the story we hear the same one she meant to tell?

Both Austin's speech act theory and Todorov's emphasis on the different levels of meaning in a narrative allow us to see that there is a lively flow between the teller and the listener of a story and between what is in the text and what is evoked by the text. As discussed in Chapter 5, it is important to hold several types of meaning in mind when examining the early development of young children's stories. Their stories unfold in a profoundly social way, and therefore the dynamic among what is said, what is meant, what is heard, and what is understood is of great significance. This constellation, in constant flux, holds the key to the myriad meanings their stories can reveal to us.

This set of ideas, taken together with those about what a narrative is, suggests guidelines for identifying and illuminating the stories of young children. First, to be considered stories, narratives need to fulfill certain criteria. Stories must describe or evoke events placed in time and space, must convey some sense of what is usual and unusual, must contain or refer to some point of drama, a sense of tension, and/or a transformation.

A story must also convey some sense of subjective experience, either by describing the author's or hero's consciousness or by including a protagonist capable of intentions and feelings. Stories balance a relationship among author, text, and audience. They may contain all of these elements of narrative and achieve these criteria more or less explicitly. At the less well-formed or explicit end of the continuum, they may be narratives without qualifying as full-fledged stories. A child's story may only evoke or approximate the characteristics (such as reference to subjective experience, and the recognizable voice of the author) that we assume are explicit and well developed in the stories of adult authors.

A second set of ideas directs our attention toward understanding the different spheres of potential meaning in a child's story—the child's explicit story, the meanings it evokes in her, the story that the listener hears, and the meaning that story evokes for the listener. We can map out these different worlds of meaning for any given story, and these mappings can be applied to the variety of types of stories that children tell.

4

$\blacklozenge$

The Kinds of Stories Children Tell

$\blacklozenge$

A 4-year-old girl announces to her mother, "I'm gonna tell you a real true story, and I just made it up." Children tell a wide range of stories, from the briefest snippets told in the flow of family conversation to long accounts of events with characters, plots, and elaborate descriptions. They most often use the narrative form to tell about personal experiences. But they also construct fictions and, in early childhood, often appear to slide seamlessly back and forth between fact and fiction. As they enter middle childhood, they are increasingly likely to make clear distinctions between "true" stories and made-up ones.

Let us talk about three kinds of stories that children tell: stories of personal experience, stories told collaboratively with others, and fictional stories. This way of grouping children's stories captures the salient characteristics of developing narratives. Drawing on the ideas presented in the last chapter, we can see that stories can be understood both in terms of their textual characteristics, the relationship between the narrator and his or her audience, and the different layers of meaning in any given story. Children use the story form to explore a wide range of ideas and experiences.

Stories of Personal Experience

◆

Among the most important types of stories people tell are stories about their own experiences. We tell stories about our personal experiences to relive them, share our experiences with others, communicate information about ourselves to others, master emotions connected to the experiences, and solve cognitive puzzles. What are these stories like, and when and where are they constructed?

It is clear from Emily's monologues (see Chapter 2) that as children we begin telling ourselves about our personal experiences from a very early age. Peggy Miller and Lois Sperry have shown in their recordings of Baltimore families that children also tell their parents about personal experiences from an early age. My own research has demonstrated that children as young as 16 months talk about the past with their parents. Very young children talk with each other about their personal experiences as well. The developmental psychologist Alison Preece tape-recorded three children on their way to and from preschool every day for eighteen months. Of the fourteen different types of narratives she identified, personal anecdotes were the most prevalent, accounting for 70 percent of the stories the children told.

When children tell stories about their own experience
to themselves, it tends to be for the purpose of mentally
organizing events, gaining some kind of cognitive and/or
emotional mastery over experience, or working out an emotional or cognitive puzzle. At first these stories are likely
to be about routine events, although these routines may
initially be as interesting to the child and as replete with
to-be-mastered material as is the greatest mystery to an adult.
These stories are typically told in advance of the experience as
a kind of planning narrative, or they're told at bedtime as a
kind of summary of and reflection on the day's events. The
organization of experience (what came first, what happened
next, and so on) drives the narrative, as does the mental push
to set experience in a time and space framework.

Although routine events provide the basis for building
up a repertoire of scripts, and thus pave the way for the
development of more general storytelling abilities, they typically are not the basis for the stories children tell to others
about their personal experience. The stories we first tell to
others tend instead to be about more novel experiences.
For instance, in a nursery school where children are asked to
begin the day by relating what they ate for breakfast, children
might avoid the perfunctory response of "waffles," or "eggs,"
or "I don't know" and spontaneously tell about something
unusual that happened: "This morning my mom gave me Rice
Krispies with lots and lots of sugar. And you know what
the snap crackle pop said to me? It said, 'Soon it's going to be
summer, and I'm the strongest boy in the world.'"

Even very young children are aware of the presence of a
spectator or an audience, and that the unusual may capture the
listener's interest. This awareness leads them to choose subject
matter that is more novel than the routines they might narrate
to themselves while going to bed and to highlight what's

exciting about it. For instance, here 3 $^{1}/_{2}$-year-old Lee is telling his 6-year-old brother Dustin about what happened to him at a birthday party:

> *Well, you see, first I had the water gun, and I was shoot-*
> *ing Chris and Tony. And they didn't have any water guns,*
> *and they were like ahhh. And then I ran around and hid*
> *behind the barn, and they were looking for me, and then*
> *they got me, and they were holding on to me, and they*
> *kept shooting me with the gun like 100 times, and I was*
> *laughing so hard.*

The story has a protagonist, who is also the author, typical of any personal anecdote. It is action oriented, and like many young children's stories, it is spare, including very little in the way of embellishments, descriptive detail, explicit interpretations of events, and only one sentence that suggests subjective experience ("and they were like ahhh"). There is no explicit comment on the meaning of the story, nor any evaluation of how the story should be taken by the listener.

Adults, by contrast, often include explicit interpretation or evaluation in their descriptions of events. "God. I had the worst day. First I got a flat tire, then I lost the notes for my meeting, and then. . . ." Such evaluations often prepare and guide the listener about the significance or value of the story—in this case, the reasons why the teller is so strung out. But young children, so eager to share experience with their peers, typically make an implicit assumption that the meaning of the story is transparent. In a story like the water gun fight, the action is told very directly, without explicit comment on its meaning. And yet we know that the author experienced the fight as funny and exciting. He shares his experience as he experienced it. The roles of author and protagonist are nearly identical; the distancing of authorship is minimal or is not reflected in the structure of the text. Setting the scene for the audience is not nearly as important for the child as conveying the experience that he has had.

When young children recount their personal experiences, they typically do not explicitly distinguish between an event and their experience of it. The two levels of reality are merged. As children begin to develop an awareness of the difference between a seemingly objective account of events and their own view of those events, they often present their perspective in encapsulated comments at the beginning or end of their account. For instance, a young child might say of a trip to the lake, "We swam, and the water was cold cold cold. Sandra splashed me but I splashed her right back," whereas an older child might say, "We went swimming. It was great. The water felt freezing, but you got used to it after a while. The younger kids were splashing like crazy. They both ended up crying. But mostly it was a really fun day." Sometimes the older child's dawning awareness of the difference between recounting events and conveying personal perspective leads to the construction of less evocative dynamic stories. By offering the facts and then an extrapolated interpretation or comment on them, the teller may drain the description of its communicative force.

The personal anecdotes that follow illustrate how this distinction emerges as children get older. As you see, the youngest children, two 5 year olds, integrate what happened with what they know, merge what they saw or felt with an account of events.

My best memory is my friend. Her name is Amanda. I made a snowman with her. I went to the big E with her. I

*went sledding with her. She is my best friend. She lives
across the street from me.*

*My best memory was when Grandpa was in the war. He
dropped torpedoes on ships.*

Next, a 7 year old recounts a memory, but unlike the 5 year
olds, he places the event in a temporal context and separates
what happened from what he felt about it:

*I remember when I was at camp, and Nick, my best
friend, came over to my house for the night and we had
lots of fun. I liked it a lot.*

Finally, an account written by a 9 year old provides a clear
anecdote and a clear commentary on an event, including her
own experience of the event and an objective perspective on
her role in it:

*I remember when I was in my cousin Margo's wedding
and I was a flower girl. It was lots of fun. I wore a white
dress with a pink sash. I had a white headband with little
flowers and bows on it. I looked pretty.*

Young children tell wonderful stories about their past, in
their own way. But until recently most research tended to portray children's first attempts at recounting personal experience
as illogical, nonsequential, and lacking in both accuracy and
completeness. When researchers have asked children between
the ages of 3 and 9 to tell about a past experience, they have
usually been interested in assessing the children's memory
capacity and ability to organize information. The research is

often premised on the investigator's having had some outside knowledge of the event being recounted (a documented trip to a museum or a zoo, an experience at home that the parent had also given an account of, and the like). Thus, the emphasis of the analysis has often been on how much the children can remember, whether they describe the sequence of events accurately, and whether they describe the events as they really were. Important as such analysis are, they tend to overlook the effectiveness of these early personal narratives and their aesthetic characteristics.

Although young children's autobiographical narratives are often incomplete, idiosyncratically organized, and uneven in their level of detail, they are also interesting to read or hear, highly personal and specific. They can be surprisingly successful at evoking a vivid experience of the event in the mind of the reader. In this, they are often more like the narratives found in good literature than those contained in case histories or court testimony.

The recent focus on children as court witnesses, and the possibility that children embellish or fabricate remembered events, suggest that there are at least two modes in which children recount the past, or at least two modes in which we can scrutinize their verbalization of personal memories. We may look for how accurate their accounts are (relevant when children are acting as witnesses, for instance), but it is equally important to appreciate and understand their creative and aesthetic skills in telling stories that may or may not capture the sequence or details of a real event.

The author's ability to give the reader a sense that he or she can experience or feel what the author has experienced is often what elevates an account of a memory to the status of literature. Children may produce many stories that fail as good testimony but succeed as evocative tales. And although these stories may not be useful for ascertaining the actions of others (as would be needed in testimony), they may be very rich as products of creative development and as windows into the child's inner life.

The variety of ways in which children may express meaning and evoke experience in an audience when recounting their personal memories can be illustrated by the results of a study I conducted a few years ago. I asked twenty 7 year olds during the second week of school to write their autobiographies. After a brief group discussion of what this might include, children eagerly pursued the project and came up with a range of autobiographical styles. They organized their experiences in a variety of ways, chose differing kinds of details to bring their memories alive, and used an assortment of aesthetic devices to create a strong image in their reader's mind.

The children used three different approaches to organize experiences into an autobiography. Two of the twenty children gave conventional chronological accounts of their past. Much of their material was not recounted as a series of episodes per se but consisted of remembered information, based on what they had been told by adults. For instance:

> When I was born I was 20 inches tall. I was born on
> November 26, 1978. It was 4:20 in the morning. I was
> born at Fairview hospital. My hair was black, but now
> it's blond. My first word was plant. I said, "Plant, plant."
> When I was one my Mom and Pop got divorced.

Nine of the autobiographies consisted of scene descriptions from the child's past that had no apparent chronological order. In these examples, which exemplify this "collection" approach, only the core or essence of the event is named:

My dad got stuck in a storm and I was nervous. He came
back the other day. I was walking my dog and my dog
pulled me. I broke my arms. I go sailing lots of times. I
was skipping and I tripped on a big rock and I got rocks
in my knee. I visited my friend Janine in New Mexico.

We went to Italy and we had a good time. We went in
summer. We went to an amusement park. We went swim-
ming in the mountain pool. The water was cold and
clean. We drove through the Alps and we saw people on
motorcycles. They were racing.

Nothing is said to orient the reader in terms of life context or even to show how the scenes are related to one another. The focus in each component is the experiencing subject, the "I," which is what creates the sense of continuity. Memorable actions, objects, and feelings are named, yet there is little in the way of scene depiction and no elaboration. The impression created is that of a list of remembered events, a collection of snapshots chosen for their individual interest rather than for their relation to one another.

In the third kind of formulation, the children described a structured series of scenes (nine autobiographies fell into this category). In these autobiographies, the scenes conveyed are chronologically arranged, but the order serves more as a vehicle for the scene depictions than as a basis for the development of a life story. The child seems either to have chosen interesting or meaningful scenes and then arranged them chronologically or recalled events (or information about them) in chronological order, lifting out appealing scenes as he scanned. The relation between the scenes is not articulated, although it can often be mentally interpolated by the interpreting reader as the narrative emerges.

When I was born my sister had a best friend Lynne and we went on vacation on the beach it was hot and I was very happy because I was in the sea and my sis and her best friend Lynne were taking me by both hands and swinging me by both hands and swinging me back and forth and I tried to squiggle out because I was afraid of the waves and when I ran and ran my feet were getting too wet and my sis and Lynne were laughing so hard that I started laughing too and when my mom took me up for a nap I was laughing so hard that I could not go to sleep. When I was 1 years old I once was outside and I was in the clothes basket and it was funny.

The two scenes are ostensibly related chronologically. The first scene, however implausible, is supposedly from birth and the next scene from his first year. But the more compelling connection is thematic. Both scenes are meant to be funny and involve experiences of place. Thus, the attempt at chronology serves as an external structure, and the author's view of the meaning of the events drives the actual descriptions and selections.

In this next example, the author conveys personal meaning through the choice and sequencing of simple descriptions. He does not articulate the connections between events, nor does he elaborate on the meaning of these events. Yet a distinct personal history is conveyed:

I had a car that I rode around the house. When my Mom and Dad had a fight I pushed them away from each other. Then my Dad moved to Albany. When I was a little kid every time I sat in the tub I was afraid I would go down the drain.

Children are rarely comprehensive in their account of life events. Nor do they typically focus only on major experiences. They often go back and forth between large and small episodes from their past, and like many good authors, choose the odd or small experience to convey who they are and what they have experienced. They can be "accurate" without being encyclopedic. While this may sometimes cause their stories to seem inadequate as full reports of the past, it makes their accounts more revealing than a dry and exhaustive account would.

Although certain conventional anchor points are often included in children's narratives (birth, first day of school, learning to walk, the death of a relative), the narrative emphasis tends to be more on idiosyncratic details and descriptions of vivid scenes. Here is an example:

> I lived at my Mom and Dad's. My two brothers lived
> with us. We lived in Stockbridge. When I was 3 I tried to
> save my friend and I fell in the pool and almost drowned.
> Then my brother tried to save me, then my other brother
> tried to save him. Then my mother cannon-balled in and
> saved us all. She made a tidal wave, man.

This account begins with conventionally important but static information. The dynamic part of the autobiography involves an episode that, while exciting, is not, from a conventional perspective, central to his life story. Like the personal account typical of children at this age, the description is concrete and action oriented. Actions, almost always involving the narrator, are the central focus of the recollections. Other people, places, and feelings are mentioned in relation to something the rememberer did or experienced. The reader knows what happened but is rarely given an amplification of the event. For instance:

> *When I was 2 I had my first bike and I rode my bike and I rode it to a beautiful flower and picked it and the roots came out my dad was very mad. When I was four I made a face on a pumpkin and on the same day I built a nest out of pine needles.*

There is little in the way of explicit embellishment or interpretation here. Personal meaning comes through the choice of details offered, their ordering, and the ordering of the scenes described. Editing rather than elaborating is the primary means of constructing or communicating the meaning of experience.

Two things are paradoxically true of the way children convey actions and events: (1) they cause the reader to experience an event as the author might have experienced or reexperienced the event; and (2) this emphasis on reconstructing experience is completely implicit.

In order to identify what children are doing in these autobiographical stories that gives them such a sense of immediacy, some students and I looked at how pronouns and verbs were used to convey perspective. Over half of the events were described in the personal active past (I did, I felt, I heard, I saw). Less than a third began with more ongoing, passive constructions "I was" or "I had," and only a small number revealed any sense of reflection, interpretation, or subjectivity, by beginning with "It looked to me," "It felt," or "It sounded." Thus, the overall quality of the narratives was one of directly experienced specific action. The great majority of events were specified as occurring within a defined period of time (an hour, an afternoon), whereas approximately 20 percent were about things that happened over undefined periods of time. Again this adds to the quality of immediacy.

The structure of the children's descriptions often paralleled the structure of their experience of that event. For instance:

I saw a bear eating something. He was eating a fish.

I was at a picnic and I had some ice cream. It fell on my blanket. It fell on my foot too.

My best memory is when I was on a boat. I was seeing the Statue of Liberty. It was deep deep water.

In these three examples the sequence of information parallels the sequence of experience. The sentences act as a kind of camera. First the author describes the big scene, then zooms in on a detailed portion of the scene. And, like a scene filmed in this way, the audience experiences the event as the author may have originally.

In an attempt to understand the narratives in terms of their effect on a reader, two adults read the accounts. Each aspect of an event or item of information was categorized as either an inside or an outside statement. Inside statements were all those descriptions and propositions that were told from the experiencer's point of view and simultaneously allowed the listener or reader to see that event or information from the narrator's perspective. Inside statements included things like "When I was born I was cold"; "But then I saw they were not taking me out to play, they were taking me out to eat smushed banana." Outside statements, of which there were twice as many as inside statements, were those that placed both the experiencer and the listener outside of the event, for example, "I went to Disneyland when I was four"; "My mother was there when he died."

Many good adult writers, when writing about their own past, have said that they are trying to experience things as children do. They suggest that directness, simplicity, and sharpness are childlike characteristics that they try to achieve in their writing. Virginia Woolf said about writing her memoirs, "I reach a state where I seem to be watching things happen as if I were there. That is, I suppose that my memory supplies what I had forgotten so that it seems as if it were happening independently, though I am really making it happen." This captures what many young children do as well. Woolf also said about writing of her past, "[people] were caricatures; they were very simple; they were immensely alive. They could be made with three strokes of a pen."

In looking at the autobiographies of 7 year olds, it becomes apparent that the qualities that make children's narratives seem immature and even inadequate by traditional standards are the same qualities that make them interesting to hear and effective at creating experience in the mind of a listener. A growing number of researchers have begun to identify the techniques by which children communicate the personal meaning of their stories.

Karen Malan, for example, a South African researcher, has tape-recorded Afrikaaner children telling an adult stories about past experiences. The children, who chose exciting personally significant events in their lives to talk about, were marvelously inventive in using the form of the story to convey meaning. Three-year-old J., for instance, effectively uses repetition in his story (the line numberings are Malan's):

1   our dog is dead
2   the dog knocked the van over
3   our dog is buried

4   and the car then knocks him over
5   then the blood comes out
6   then the blood pours out
7   then he goes buried

8   then Balie's going to take him to the doctor
9   Balies going to take him to the doctor
10   and then Balie cried
11   that dog is dead

These children use a variety of literary techniques to convey meaning. In this example, repetition (lines 1 and 11, 3 and 7, 5 and 6, 8 and 9) is used for impact, to reveal and communicate the power of these details and images for the storyteller. Although we cannot assess the young storytellers' intent when they use techniques such as repetition, we can see a compelling parallel in listener effect with the techniques adult authors use to create images and convey emphasis. For instance, Alice Walker, in her poem "We Have a Beautiful Mother" begins each stanza with the line "We have a beautiful mother." It may be that what changes through development is the conscious awareness and deliberate use of these expressive techniques.

As children get older, their stories about personal experiences change in other ways as well. They are more likely to include material on other people, a change that reflects an increasing interest in the social world. In *The Beginnings of Social Understanding*, for example, Judy Dunn writes that during children's third year their narratives about other people increase dramatically. She collected too few to even analyze in children between 24 and 26 months, whereas by the time they were 36 months old the average number of narrative comments about others had increased to approximately ninety. She argues that this change parallels children's increased curiosity about other people, manifested in their increased number of questions about others.

Children, like adults, want to tell stories about exciting things that have happened to them. Achieving this often involves telling stories that are a mixture of fact and fiction. Sticking to a purely fictional or factual account is not of primary concern to most young storytellers, or, for that matter, to good novelists. Finding a form that conveys one's meaning or experience takes precedence over strict adherence to fact or fantasy.

As children move from toddlerhood to school age, they increasingly distinguish between spheres of experience. They begin to distinguish real life from what is imagined and what they have learned from stories from what they have learned from direct experience. Children's narratives reflect their emerging cognitive differentiation of spheres of experience. But children also use the story form to clarify for themselves the difference between what they have made up and what they have experienced. A mother of a 4 year old told me that in the car she and her son make up stories together. One day her son, Adam, began a story: "Once upon a time there was a little boy and he had a big dog, and an old cat." The mother continued: "Yes, and they lived near the sea and the little boy had a unicorn," at which point Adam interrupted indignantly, "But I don't have a unicorn."

In the last few years there has been an intensifying concern over the nature of children's recollection of earlier experiences of abuse. The work of researchers such as Elizabeth Loftus has shown us that in fact children often do confuse or blend what they experienced with what they have been told and what they imagine. In one of Loftus's more famous studies, young children were told by an older child or an adult that they had experienced a brief and scary separation from their parent at a store a number of weeks before. Although at first the subjects were dubious about or resistant to the existence of such an event, over time they came not only to accept that this event had happened to them, but they began adding their own details to its "recollection."

While this phenomenon of false memory complicates the important task of using children as witnesses in abuse cases, it fits with an understanding of the narrative form as one in which different types of reality can be interwoven. As we get older, we may be more able to make these distinctions clear in our stories and in our minds, though it is equally clear that few of us consistently and reliably can sort out what we think happened from what really happened. Narratives are, by their very nature, a personal and interpretive product of a constructive process.

Shared Personal Anecdotes

Children not only tell stories about personal experiences to others, they tell stories of personal experiences *with* others. They co-narrate with parents, siblings, and peers, at home, in day care, on the playground, in school. Perhaps the simplest form of collaboration is one in which a familiar adult, through questions and reactions, encourages a child to elaborate and essentially revise her story.

Five-year-old Erika and her friend Anna are enjoying milk and cookies around the table with Anna's grandfather, when

Erika says, "My father caught a horse yesterday. He was running down the street and my father gave him a bite of his chocolate chip cookie. They came and took him to the stable."

The grandfather then asked Anna some questions about the story. His questions led to the following additions: Erika's father apparently had left the house and was walking along eating a chocolate chip cookie. A horse came running down Broadway. (A stable for police horses is quite close by.) Erika's father held up the cookie, and the horse stopped to nibble it. Some policemen ran after the horse and took it back to the stable. Apparently a similar incident had occurred some time earlier, involving another runaway police horse.

Erika's original story hits the highlights. It begins with the main point, the hook; she gives the events some sequence, a little dramatic resolution. The interesting part of this is that Erika's narrative is perfectly accurate and quite neat in its original form. But in response to questions from her audience, it grows and becomes a somewhat different memory for her, and a somewhat different story for her audience, when she tells it again. In addition, as shown in Chapter 5, Erika learns in the process something about what kinds of information adults think is interesting and important and want her to include in her stories.

Preschool-age children typically do a great deal of co-narrating in their families, but this seems to fall off dramatically once children get to school. In *The Meaning Makers*, Gordon Wells shows that at least in England not only are collaborative conversations less frequent in school settings, but when they do occur they tend to be shorter, sparer in detail, and less often child initiated. The potential for schools to provide rich opportunities for shared story construction certainly exists, however. With the right teacher encouragement, children's interest in one another's experiences, their eagerness to engage in dialogue, and their proclivity to tell and listen to stories make them ripe for cooperative narration.

The possibilities can be illustrated by the following excerpt from a circle time discussion in an American kindergarten class. The basic plot of the story, about a moose on a lawn, was conceived and delivered by Kaitlin, the central author. But she has auxiliary authors among her peers, who help guide and shape the story. The teacher also plays a role.

Kaitlin: Guess what I saw on my lawn?

Child 1:   A dog?

Kaitlin: *(quietly)* Moose.

Teacher: Some kind of animal? Do you know what kind it is?

Child 2:   A shark!

Several others: Ohhhh!

Kaitlin: A moose. You were close, David.

Child 3:   Well, what was it doing on your lawn?

Child 2:   I said shark.

Kaitlin: Nothin . . . it wasn't doing nothing. It was just eating grass.

Child 2:   Know what I said, Steve? Know what I said, Brian? I said a shark.

Child 4:   Why was it even there then?

Child 3:   I knew it.

Kaitlin: It was a hog.

Teacher: Excuse me, boys and girls, I don't think we can hear if we're talking.

Kaitlin: He was eating my I, he was eating, um, um, our backyard grass and well, I opened the wind . . . I well, I ran downstairs I told my Dad, "Dad, Dad there's a moose in our, in our um lawn, and it's eating the grass" and the—

Child 2:   Was he giving it any, was he . . .

Kaitlin: And then he, and then he ran out the back stairs and he said "Oh Kaitlin, how'd you find this, hmmm?"

Teacher: David has another question for you.

Child 2:   Kaitlin, what did you do? Was it cutting the grass and your Dad didn't need to do your lawn mower?

Kaitlin: Well, see the moose was eating the grass.

Child 5:   Oh, so he ran in and got his shotgun and killed it.

Child 2:   Do you ever go hiking in the woods?

Kaitlin: Yeah. Well not hunting, not hunting.

Child 3:   Shshs. shhh.

Child 4:   She said hiking.

Kaitlin: David, Davey, David, not hunting, just like—

Teacher: Okay, David.

Kaitlin: Not moose, deer, yeah.

Teacher: I think what David's saying is that if you had a moose that ate grass, your Dad wouldn't need to mow his, mow the lawn because the moose could eat all the grass.

Kaitlin: Well, it's not my pet moose, it just came out of the woods.

Child 1:   How close do you live to the woods?

Child 2:   I know I have a big wood by my house.

This story, central aspects of which may have been made up by Kaitlin, definitely crosses the boundary between the transactional and the spectator, types of discourse discussed in Chapter 3. This example illustrates the idea that a story need not contain verifiable events, experienced by the group, in order for several children to collaborate in the telling of it. What is the story that was just told, and how did it get told? The story is this:

Kaitlin saw a moose on her lawn.

She told her Dad.

He ran outside, saw it too, and asked her how she had found it.

The moose was eating the grass, so maybe her Dad wouldn't have to cut the grass.

The implication is that a pet moose, which this wasn't, could be a lawn mower.

The story led to several possible detours and elaborations, for instance, about hunting in the woods, the differences between deer and moose, and how close Kaitlin lives to the woods. This is typical of stories told by groups of young children. The story is like a path that contains dead ends and branch roads, a kind of verbal choose-your-own-adventure.

The children direct the content of the story with their questions and their interest. For instance, when Child 3 asks, "What was it doing on your lawn?" he is guiding the story towards the moose's action rather than the responses of people in the story. In such ways participants can shape a story just by their questions, even if they were not part of the experience, and can thus contribute no actual information. The participants can also provide some of the stylistic or formal characteristics of the narrative. For instance, when Kaitlin opens with "Guess what I saw on my lawn?" the children begin an exciting guessing game about what kind of animal she might have seen. An accomplished adult storyteller might try to build this tension into the narrative, enticing the listener to anticipate a climax. But Kaitlin may not yet be able to integrate this into her narrative on her own. Luckily, she has confederates who build up the dramatic tension through their questions and guesses, and who savor that tension ("Know what I said, Brian? I said a shark.").

Beyond the development of group narrative, Wells notes that there's a further value in this activity for individual children:

> The children are contributing freely from their own experience. And as they narrate those experiences to others they are, perhaps for the first time, discovering their significance for themselves. These are the conditions that foster language development: when one has something important to say, and other people are interested in hearing it. It is then that language and thinking most fully interpenetrate in the struggle to make meanings that capture what one has observed and understood and communicate that understanding to others.

Children collaborate not only based on one person's experience, they can also do so based on shared experiences. Jonathan Kozol gives a devastating example. In *Savage Inequalities,* he reports the following conversation with a small group of children ranging in age from 7 to 9, in East St. Louis, Illinois:

> The children regale me with a chilling story as we stand beside the marsh. Smokey says his sister was raped and murdered and then dumped behind his school. Other children add more details: Smokey's sister was 11 years old. She was beaten with a brick until she died. The murder was committed by a man who knew her mother.
>
> The narrative begins when, without warning, Smokey says, "My sister has got killed."
>
> "She was my best friend," Serena says.
>
> "They had beat her in the head and raped her," Smokey says.

"She was hollering out loud," says Little Sister.

I asked them when it happened. Smokey says, "Last year." Serena then corrects him and she says, "Last week."

"It scared me because I had to cry," says Little Sister.

"The police arrested one man but they didn't catch the other," Smokey says.

Serena says, "He was some kin to her."

But Smokey objects, "He weren't no kin to me. He was my momma's friend."

"Her face was busted," Little Sister says.

Serena describes this sequence of events: "They told her go behind the school. They'll give her a quarter if she do. Then they knock her down and told her not to tell what they had did."

I ask, "Why did they kill her?"

"They was scared that she would tell," Serena says.

"One is in jail," says Smokey. "They cain't find the other."

"Instead of raping little bitty children, they should find themselves a wife," says Little Sister.

"I hope," Serena says, "her spirit will come back and get that man."

"And *kill* that man," says Little Sister.

"Give her another chance to live," Serena says.

"My teacher came to the funeral," says Smokey.

"When a little child dies, my momma say a star go straight to Heaven," says Serena.

"My Grandma was murdered," Mickey says out of the blue. "Somebody shot two bullets in her head."

I ask him, "Is she really dead?"

"She dead all right," says Mickey. "She was layin' there, just dead."

"I love my friends," Serena says. "I don't care if they have no kin to me. I care for them. I hope his mother have another baby. Name her for my friend that's dead."

"I have a cat with three legs," Smokey says.

"Snakes hate rabbits," Mickey says, again for no apparent reason.

"Cats hate fishes," Little Sister says.
"It's a lot of hate," says Smokey.

This is a moving example of the way in which children not only can work together to report an event but can co-construct a meaningful story about it, replete with connections, evaluations, moral judgments, and a sense of the emotional impact, both immediate and more distant, that the event has on them. The children manage to present a cohesive, logical, collective version of what happened, and at the same time they each interject their personal perspective—how they were related to the victim, what they feel or think about what happened. While their knowledge becomes seamless, and integrated (who did what, what happened to whom), their individual experience of the event remains to some extent separate. And yet, finally, they come together in their interpretation of the larger meaning of what happened, even collaborating on the seeming digression that leads to the moral of the story.

Smokey, Serena, and their peers told that story as a way of getting to know an interested adult, Kozol, and through doing so may have shared, for the first time, feelings and impressions with one another regarding an incident that deeply affected all of them. Children tell stories with one another, of course, for other reasons as well—negotiating a relationship, for example, or making and maintaining friends.

I have found that preschoolers use different types of story forms to serve different functions. When the point is to solve some social problem, for example, stories tend to be relatively brief, to the point, and spare in recollected detail.

Beth Ann: Can I have that cookie, because you are my
   best friend?
Penny: No. I gave you my cookie yesterday and you didn't
   give me nothing.
Beth Ann: Oh yeah? I did so. I gave you some of my Fruit
   Roll Up the other time. Last week.
Penny: Nuh, uh. You gave me that because I didn't have
   any snack that day. But it wasn't cause I was your best
   friend.
Beth Ann: Oh yeah. It was too, I gave you that Fruit Roll Up
   and now you should give me some of your cookies.
Rick: Why do you two always have to share? You always are
   sharing your snack. That's not fair. It's stupid.

When children want to make and maintain friends, on the
other hand, they engage in lengthier, more embellished descriptions that also allow for more collaborative interaction:

Tony: I went fishin' last night with my *Dad!*
Jimmy: You went what?
Tony: I went fishin' last night with my *Dad!*
Jimmy: You have a fishing pole?
Tony: Yeah, I use my brother's pole. It's *so* big. And ya
   know what? I caught a live fish!
Jimmy: Was it a shark? *(big grin)*
Tony: Yeah. I mean no, it was a, a, um a perch, my Dad said.
   And when, when he pulled the hook out there was blood all
   over the place.
Jimmy: Gross me out . . . *(they turn back to their drawings)*

Fantasy and Fiction

◆

Children's anecdotes, whether told alone or with others, draw on personal experience and make some pretense at representing things as they happened, fulfilling what psychologists Stoel-Gammon and Scliar-Cabral call the Reportative Function. What about stories that have nothing to do with experienced events, that are purely fictional? When, where, and how do children tell these kinds of stories?

Alison Preece found, in the conversations she recorded of three children on the way to and from school each day, that very few of her subjects' stories were fantasies. But she was listening to children talking to each other, in a car with her, an adult. Fantasy talk is more likely to occur under other conditions, primarily when children are alone, or actually playing with each other (rather than communicating information as would happen in a car), and in the presence of an adult only when the adult has taken on the role of story facilitator as master teacher Vivian Paley does.

When children do create fantasy stories, what are they like compared to the narratives of actual events? They tend to be more loosely organized, often without clear beginnings, middles, and ends. They tend to pick up in the middle of play. For instance, two children might be playing with action figures with only occasional comments that direct the other player, or occasional sound effects. At some point one or both children might begin talking and telling a story to accompany or expand on their gestural play with the figures. The relationship between narrative and gestural play is fluid. Children often appear to shift the emphasis of their play back and forth between words and gestures. These can be viewed as shifts in register, in much the same way that bilingual children shift between two languages. Because of this shifting back and forth the narratives themselves may appear less cohesive and neatly bounded than the thoughts behind them may actually be.

Narratives under these circumstances are less temporally organized than personal anecdotes. After all, the audience is usually either the self or a co-conspirator, so there is little need to include orienting comments such as "Once upon a time" or "In a faraway land." Instead, they tend to include a great deal of elaboration. After all, embellishment and commentary are possibilities that language offers that gesture alone cannot accomplish for most young players. You can describe subtleties of the scene, embellish the action, and articulate the meaning of the play.

Paley claims that through fantasy talk children can enter each other's worlds in a way that may not otherwise be accessible to them. Children are unlikely to speak directly and concretely to one another about their concerns and preoccupations and are unlikely to attend to this aspect of experience through gestural play alone. Through his imaginary stories, Jason, the central figure in Paley's *The Boy Who Would Be a Helicopter,* can interact with other children and also communicate with them about his feelings and ideas, learn about theirs, and incorporate theirs into his mental sphere.

All of the stories I have talked about so far in this chapter are stories told in the service of some interpersonal goal or as a part of some other activities: to communicate experience to others, to make or maintain friends, to entertain and share with a group at school, to embellish or replace other forms of play. But what about when children specifically want to, or are asked to, tell a story, when their explicit goal is simply to tell a story?

Work like that of research psychologists Nancy Stein and Tom Trabasso emphasizes the formal nature of the story task explicitly when they say to their subjects "I will tell you a story and then ask you some questions about it" or when they say "Can you tell me a story?" In fact, developmental psychologist Carol Feldman has found that elementary-school-age children are so attuned to the formal requirements of a storytelling context that they can detect and are responsive to the particular kind of story represented in the stimulus material. More significantly, they can also explain and elaborate on the stories they hear in keeping with the genre of that story. Genre here refers to different types of stories, for example, adventure stories, mysteries, parables, and so forth. Experimenters emphasize the formal nature of storytelling implicitly when they present children with a set of stories that have little else to recommend them than their story structures (the content is not relevant to anything else going on in the child's life, the story serves no other interpersonal function, and so on).

We know from this research that children get more sequential in their account of events, and more logical in the links they make in their stories and their story comprehension as they grow older. Their stories that are based on actual events become more accurate and more detailed. They include more episodes, and within the episodes they include more clauses and embed more information. The children also become better able to convey different levels of perspective and more explicit in conveying continuity (by, for example, using connectives such as "and," "because," and "so"). They are quick to adopt tricks of the storytelling trade (such as "Once upon a time"), and they use these tricks in increasing quantity over time.

When children tell stories with the only goal to fulfill the request of an experimenter or teacher, conventional story characteristics are salient. When children tell stories they are eager to tell, that are about content that matters to them, they may use conventions to help them shape the story, but they are also more likely to depart from convention in order to get across their particular fantasy or fiction. In the next example the storyteller is eager to dramatize her interest in the theme of evilness. The story vacillates between the type of conventional characteristics with which she opens her story and the unexpected, more idiosyncratic, and expressive way in which she describes the main character's awful personality.

The Wretched Princess

Once upon a time, there was this queen. She was hoping for a daughter more than anybody than they had ever known. The king said, "No, it will be too much." All the other people in the castle said "It's not too much work for us." One day she had a princess. They named the princess Jackelie. Jackelie grew up to be a princess. When she grew up they hated her. She was Evil. She was wicked. She was horrid. When she was 17 she killed both her parents. The guards tried to stop her, but all they got was their own self executed. Soon she was the only one in the castle. But she needed a husband. She married a rich boy named Hansel. The boy was treated like a donkey. Everybody hated her. When she had kids the kids didn't even speak to her. The kids didn't have any toys, and rags for clothes. They too hated their mother. When her kids were grown up the grandchildren hated her. When she died nobody came to the funeral. And they all had a party that she was dead. The End

Children develop an understanding of the underlying formula or structure of a story so well that they can enter it midstream and inject the appropriate kind of sentence. Consider this piece of fiction created by a group of 4- and 5-year-old children:

A Spider Named Elizabeth

Once upon a time there was a spider named Elizabeth. She was on her way to pick blueberries.

And on her way she saw some strawberries, so she stopped to eat some.

After Elizabeth ate some strawberries she was very tired and decided to take a nap.

Elizabeth woke up because it started raining and she was very cold. She started spinning a web.

Elizabeth worked very hard on her web until a cat came along and scared her.

So Elizabeth ran all the way to the blueberry patch where she was supposed to go in the first place.

And pick a big basket of blueberries for her grandma.

When she arrived back home her grandma made a pie for her out of the blueberries.

Each line is contributed by a different child. They are so attuned to the overall structure that each can pick up where the last child left off. Moreover, some of them use phrases that were spoken several lines back, indicating that as the story is building they are incorporating what is said into their own internal vision of the story.

What are the origins of such sophisticated understanding of storytelling? Now that we know something about the functions that storytelling serves the developing child and have a mental picture of the kind of stories children tell, we can begin to look for the earliest signs of the child's emerging storytelling abilities and trace the developmental paths along which these different kinds of stories travel.

5

◆

The Origins of Storytelling

◆

"In the last few weeks, Josh has started to do something that, to our first-time parenting eyes, is utterly delightful," the mother of a 22-month-old boy wrote to me recently. "He's started to report historical events to us—like, while eating at the dinner table, 'Josh throw rocks' 'Where?' 'Ribber' (the river) or 'Kassie (that's our dog) hop in way-back . . . Mommy's car.' It's really been fun. Up 'til now, he either narrated current events or inquired about future events (like 'go outside?') or demanded toys or other items not in direct evidence ('backhoe? Josh's backhoe?' 'Cookie? nana bread? gapes?'—banana bread, grapes).

Some time between a baby's first cries and his second birthday, he begins to know he has a past, and he wants to talk about it. How do we actually become storytellers? How do we initially learn to weave fragments of memory into a narrative and develop a sense of what a story is? And what influences these early developments?

Infant-Parent Conversations

◆

Almost from the beginning, a child's acquisition of language is a collaborative enterprise. During the first nine months or so following birth, parents tend to talk about all kinds of things with and to their children. Communities differ in terms of how much talk they address specifically to their preverbal infants. But in all cultures babies are surrounded by language, hearing and participating in the cadence and intonation of talk. At this early stage language is a somewhat undifferentiated part of the ambient environment.

Among white middle-class Americans at least, as children get closer to becoming language users themselves, parents tend to simplify both their vocabulary and syntax. Researchers such as Catherine Snow have shown that parents modify their talk to make it more accessible and useful to their novice language users. Mothers of babies who are on the cusp of talking are likely to simplify the grammar of their sentences, repeat themselves, and slow down their rate of speech. The mother's intuitive simplifications are in response to the greater likelihood that her child now will interpret some of what she says and learn from it.

Mothers and other adults assist their children in learning language in several ways, some of them amazingly subtle. Jerome Bruner has suggested the term *scaffolding* to describe the mother's role in aiding language development. The mother creates linguistic situations that require her child to keep expanding his language abilities. Mothers do this by talking to their children within highly formatted or ritualized speaking situations. For instance, talking each morning about what is for breakfast as you prepare the meal is one way to make language predictable and interpretable to your infant and toddler. As a baby learns the words his mother uses in that situation, he is then able to insert those words into a well-known linguistic routine. In this way, the mother uses the routine itself as a scaffold for language learning. So, for instance, every day a mother may say, "Let's have juice and then we will have Cheerios." There comes a day when the child can contribute by inserting the "Cheerios" in his mother's phrase.

Also, the mother scaffolds by extending the situations in which different utterances can be used appropriately by the child. For instance, that same mother may encourage her child to name Cheerios at other times: "What will we have for breakfast this morning?" or "And what did you eat at breakfast?" Parents also scaffold by requesting ever more sophisticated talk from their children. In the ideal scaffolding situation described by Bruner, the parent is in tune with the child's developmental level and therefore talks in a way that demands linguistic skills that are always a bit beyond what the child is currently doing, but not beyond his reach. So the parent might ask, "And who came over to have Cheerios with you this morning?" or, "And what did you do after breakfast?" but would not ask, "What kind of food is Cheerios?"

Parents also scaffold by elaborating and clarifying what their child does say. When the child says, "I see Grandaddy," the parent might respond, "Oh, you saw Grandaddy?" repeating what the child says but putting the verb into the correct tense. The parent starts from where the child is, inching him along to the next stage of language sophistication. This is something like the way we might teach young kids to swim. We hold out our arms and urge them to swim toward us, but if they are doing a fine job we step backward, all the while beckoning and encouraging them to "swim to me."

For many years, it was believed that toddlers only talked about what they were seeing, doing, and feeling at the moment, the "here and now." Grace de Laguna and Heinz Werner, among others, claimed that the child did not differentiate between language and the feelings, objects, and actions that language named. It was thought that toddlers did not use language to describe experience but, rather, that language was, for the young child, part and parcel of her experience along with actions. Toddlers, even preschoolers, it was believed, did not talk about things that were not happening at the moment, did not refer to objects or feelings or events in the past or future, or even existing objects set in another place. Most researchers still agree that toddlers talk a great deal about the here and now. But in recent years, they have demonstrated that children do talk about events elsewhere more frequently than was formerly believed, and that even before toddlers are talking about the past on their own, their parents are doing it, first for them, then with them.

In the first years, a lot of the stories children participate in are ones they hear their family tell, about what just happened, what happened a long time ago, and what might happen in the future.

Hello little sugar plum. You had a lousy night last night, didn't you? Yes, you woke up five times. Poor little mushroom. You didn't like those strawberries, did you? They gave your tummy a bad little ache, didn't they?

And you couldn't sleep, could you? Yes. We had a bad night, didn't we?

In this example a little girl's father tells her what her night was like. He weaves the events of her night into a story that both of them can hear. He sequences the episodes, he links cause and effect (the strawberries caused her stomachache), and he interprets her experience.

Let's put on your warm boots because we are going to the park later with Cynthia and Robby. Yeah, we are. First we're going to have breakfast and then we're going to put on our warmest clothes and go in the stroller over to the park and meet Cynthia and Robby. And you and Robby can play in the sandbox the way you love to. Yeah, and maybe we will bring your favorite truck, and you and Robby can load it with sand and drive it over to the pond and dump it. That's going to be fun. I can hardly wait, can you?

This mother turns her plan of activities for the morning into a story. She describes what the sequence of events will be, highlights what may turn out to be special for the child (bringing your favorite truck, loading it with sand), and describes what the emotional tone is likely to be (that's going to be fun, I can hardly wait).

In both of these examples the parent turns the child's experience, in one case past, in the other future, into a story and tells the story to the child. The child is mainly the audience for, rather than an equal verbal contributor to, these earliest stories. They serve as precursors to, and models for, the stories the child will eventually construct on her own. They show her how to organize experience so that it has continuity and sequence, in a framework of time. Perhaps most importantly, they give the child a sense of the meaning of experience, they show that each event as it is talked about can be interpreted, and that we guide our experience of events with the words we choose to describe and share them.

Although in these early stories children may be relatively silent partners, they're partners nonetheless. The developmental psychologist Colwyn Trevarthen has shown that babies as young as 4 months and their mothers share in the contemplation of objects. The baby looks at a red ball lying on the floor. He looks up at his mother, then back at the ball, then back at his mother again. What he sees on her face is part of how he experiences the ball. Trevarthen suggests that there is an important intersubjective quality to the way in which babies first observe and think about stable objects in the world. Social and cognitive development are interwoven; grasping the physical world occurs through social interaction.

Slightly older children, as they begin to understand the language of stories, also often experience events by participating in them with a parent. By hearing stories about the world, people and events become objects of thought, allowing us to reflect upon them. When the parent—typically, first the mother—describes experience, she is creating an object of contemplation and inviting her child to share in this contemplation. As the mother describes an excursion she and the child have recently made together, she is painting a verbal canvas. Having finished, she stands back and invites her child to consider it with her. Now they not only have the verbal painting (the story), but they can look again and again at it, comment on it, even change it in the light of new understanding.

As Jerome Bruner has suggested, making experience meaningful involves interpreting it. Stories are an interpretation, a version, of experience. The mother, in telling about shared experience, is highlighting for her child what is meaningful, enjoyable, worth talking about.

Parent-child collaboration in talk about the past is similar to other kinds of linguistic collaboration that occur between parents and children. For instance, what parent and child do together with syntax, dialogue, and vocabulary predicts and leads to what the child can do on his or her own at a later stage. But collaborating to describe the past also has some special characteristics and implications.

Recently scholars have acknowledged the unique status of talk about the past. Language about the "there and then," as Jacqueline Sachs calls it, forms the basis of our more general ability to use language to conjure up nonexistent experience (either because it happened at another place or time, or because it was fictional). Talk about the past constitutes one kind of memory, and it may pave the way for all kinds of storytelling. Researchers thus have begun to focus on the language of memory as an emerging capacity in its own right, worthy of study apart from more general studies of children's language learning on the one hand and memory capacity on the other. These studies suggest that parents specifically scaffold there-and-then talk in ways that encourage the child to use language to talk about the past and to describe nonpresent experience—in other words, to tell rudimentary stories.

Between the ages of 14 and 24 months most children learn to talk. At first they tend to talk about what they are doing or about what things look and feel like. They also begin to talk about objects and events that are not present in the room, happened at an earlier time, or are likely to happen in the future. Such there-and-then talk increases dramatically between the ages of 2 and 4.

Drawing on observations from one mother-child pair over time, Sachs traced the emergence of several kinds of there-and-then talk—talk about displaced objects (not in sight of the child), events that had just happened, and events that had happened several hours, even days before. She found a close relationship between the child's talk about these aspects of experience and the mother's use of displaced reference. She argued that children are most likely to understand references to past and future events and to nonpresent objects and to talk about these things themselves when their mother's references are made within well-defined contexts and conversational routines. For example, a toddler is more likely to understand the reference to a playground she has visited with her mother earlier in the day if that reference is always brought up in the context of reading a certain book. ("See that pretty playground? We play in a playground, don't we? Did we go there this morning?") The repetitive quality of the situation makes the there-and-then reference easier for the child to interpret and try out herself.

Over time, Sachs's research showed, displaced reference required less and less contextual support. For example, when the child is older the parent might refer to the playground at times other than when reading the playground book. For every abstract use of displaced reference, Sachs concluded, a more concrete and limited form of the term preceded it. Her work suggests that mother and child interact in drawing on the environmental and conversational context to interpret and use displaced reference and that a decrease in such interaction reflects a decreasing dependence on these supports in development.

In another study of memory in early childhood, Judy Deloache looked at interactions between mothers and children that involved reference to past experiences related to objects named in a book. She analyzed the talk of children between the ages of 15 and 38 months with their mothers while looking at an illustrated alphabet book or a farm scene depicted in a book. The mothers' memory demands on their children, she found, matched the child's level. For instance, when the child already had a particular word in her vocabulary that corresponded to a picture in the book, the mother was likely to ask the child to name something pointed to in the picture. When the word was not part of the child's active vocabulary, the mother was more likely to ask for recognition, "Where is the doggy?" to which the child could respond by pointing.

As the child develops, Deloache discovered, the mother tends to ask more and more complex questions and to demand more and more verbal participation from the child. Mothers ask general knowledge questions of younger children ("What does the doggy say?") but integrate more episodic autobiographical information when talking with older children ("See the doggy? It's like the one we saw when we visited Grandma."). The work of both Sachs and Deloache suggests that parents, perhaps unconsciously, encourage their children to talk about things from the past and about upcoming events, and that this involves special kinds of questions and demands, distinguishable from other language-learning talk they engage in.

In fact, one of the things parents do through these interactions is to show their children that talk about the there and then is a particular kind of talk. By flagging it as a speech style, or special linguistic activity, they also create the possibility of transmitting their culture's particular emphasis or style of talking about the past. Bambi Scheifflin, for example, has shown that the demands made upon children by their mothers, and the kinds of talk engaged in between mothers and children, vary across cultures.

Another researcher, Ann Eisenberg, followed two young Mexican-American children from toddlerhood into their preschool years in order to trace their emerging ability to talk about nonpresent events. The children in her study tended only to refer to past events when requested to by adults, as if they had yet to learn the point of this kind of activity in and of itself. Her subjects seemed to be learning that talk about the past was a particular mental and communicative activity with its own purpose and pattern. Eisenberg suggests that the importance of memory talk may be transmitted from parent to child, and that this emphasis may also vary from one culture to another.

In another study that focuses on cultural differences in talk about the past, Mary Mullen fitted Korean and U.S. Caucasian toddlers with vests containing small microphones and tape recorders that they wore for an entire day. She found that the U.S. children and their parents referred to the past nearly three times as often as the Korean children. Furthermore, the Caucasian adults consistently reported more early childhood memories than Asian adults. She argues that autobiographical memory is more valued in Western culture, which would explain why the Caucasian families refer to the past so much more often.

Regardless of culture, several linguistic skills seem to be necessary to full-fledged talk about the past. These skills, when integrated, form the basis of narrative language. The acquisition of these skills and their integration show a rich pattern of development. During children's second year of life, for example, they typically learn how to specify time and place, to draw on nonpresent contextual cues in referring to things, to sequence events in a narrative form, and to use language in conversations. Meanwhile, their general memory capacities are expanding.

At first, young infants remember only by recognizing familiar faces, places, and events, reacting when they see something they have seen earlier, or looking dismayed when something is different from what it was before. But by the time they are 2 years old they can recall things that are no longer present. They can reenact previous experiences, name objects that are missing, and ask for things from the past. These memories can be cued by a wide variety of stimuli and can increasingly be recalled at will. While the development of memory talk is concurrent with more general language acquisition on the one hand and the growth of memory on the other, it also constitutes its own developmental path.

The Social Origins of Memory

If parents help their children talk about the past, does the parent-child interaction have any effect on the development of the child's memory of past experiences? That is, do parents just teach children how to talk about the past, or does their input actually shape the child's memories and/or descriptions of past experience?

The British psychologist Frederic Bartlett, whose work is briefly discussed in Chapter 1, was among the first to develop the notion that memory has a social basis. Bartlett's theory of memory, put forth in the 1930s, suggested that we reconstruct past episodes or stories around ongoing schemas we have for particular experiences. These schemas, or predictive structures, are to some extent culturally derived. Bartlett's work with folktales and their repetition within a culture showed that cultural categories are drawn upon and strengthened by their use in reconstructing past events and stories. He argued that when individuals or groups of people recall stories and events, they change the stories in certain predictable ways: They blend, condense, omit, and invent elements. The form in which the memory is expressed reflects, in the case of the individual, personal history, and in the case of a culture, social organization and cultural priorities. He stressed the transforming role the process of memory plays on experience as it is stored and then recalled by the individual and/or by the social group.

Bartlett's view that the telling of stories within a community constitutes a form of social memory has been seminal to current views of the interpersonal nature of many cognitive activities. Although most people tend to think of memory as a purely intraindividual process, his studies suggest that memory is also an interpersonal process.

The idea that mental processes occur between people as well as within the individual was being explored during the same time by a Soviet psychologist, Lev Vygotsky. Articulating an idea he called the "zone of proximal development," he argued that there were two measures of a child's cognitive ability in any given domain or on any given task. The child could reach the first level on his own without any help or instruction. The child could achieve the second level of performance with the instruction of an adult or a more competent peer. Thus, the distance between these two levels of performance is the zone of proximal development. Vygotsky argued that what the child could do with help at one point, he would be able to do on his own with further development. Interpersonal achievement, in other words, preceded and predicted intrapersonal achievement.

Vygotsky's theory underscores the importance of viewing activities such as narrative remembering within an interpersonal and social framework. The input of the "other"—in many cases, a parent—is central to understanding what the child can do and is learning to do. Family interactions may not only be the context in which children's thinking develops; they may also help shape how the child thinks. Irving Sigel and Luis Laosa recorded young children at home with their parents and showed that parents initiate and direct the child's representation of experience.

> The mother says to the child, "Where have you been?" The child responds, "I have been to school." The mother asks, "What did you do in school today?" The child responds by describing an array of activities. The mother's queries prompt the child to reconstruct previous experiences and, in the process of this reconstruction, the child re-presents those experiences to himself or herself.

One of the most intriguing problems posed by this focus on interpersonal influences on development concerns how best to identify and describe abilities, such as budding narrative ones, that may not reside within the child alone but between the child and the parent. Ronald Scollon did a marvelous analysis in which he showed that parents and children construct full grammatical sentences across turns. Scollon calls this kind of joint performance "vertical construction" because the full ability occurs across verbal turns, represented down the page in transcripts of conversations, as opposed to within one speaker's turn, which would be represented horizontally in a transcript. He suggests that in dialogues certain kinds of language formats are co-constructed. Each participant uses his turn to contribute to the full grammatical form. With the young child, the parent will contribute the missing parts of the construction. Often the parent's contribution causes the child to add to her own utterance in a way that makes the child's utterance (as a whole) more complex grammatically.

Child: Soup.
Mother: What are you talking about?
Child: Drink soup.

The mother's request for clarification causes the child to add to her sentence. In this way the child and the mother co-construct full grammatical phrases across the conversation. Linguistic turns provide a way for parent and child to share in a psychological process, and they also provide a way for us to see the shared nature of some aspects of development. Before a child can construct narratives on her own, she may construct stories, and germs of stories, in conversations with her parents.

Not only are conversations the site of memory talk, they may also shape those descriptions of the past and, therefore, those memories. Can children describe the past in conversations in a way that goes beyond what they can do alone? Do those shared descriptions of the past shape the child's way of talking about memories and telling stories? In order to look at this more closely, I conducted a study several years ago of the way mothers and children talked about the past. Our initial aim was to explore how mothers helped their children learn to talk about the past. We selected four mother-child pairs and visited their homes every two weeks for a five-month period, from the time the children were 18 or 19 months old until they were 24 months old. During these visits we recorded every-thing that was said by mother and child.

In addition to looking at a few families in depth over an extended period of time, we wanted to have a broader base of comparison. For this we made a single visit to the homes of eighteen mother-child pairs. At the time of the visit six of the children were 18 months, six were 24 months, and six were 30 months old. Prior to the observation session, we asked mothers to refer to three different events from the past, using three different types of cues. The parent could initiate a conver-sation by pointing to a photograph and talking about some event depicted in the picture, she could point to or hold up an object or comment on one the child was playing with and talk about some event involving that object, or she could talk about an experience related to something mentioned in their ongoing conversation ("Do you want to have noodles for lunch today? Remember the other day when we made our own noodles with Grandma's noodle machine? That was funny, wasn't it?").

References to the past in these interactions ranged from single-utterance descriptions by the mother to long conversa-tions between mother and child that included a large variety of information about an event. We observed a host of differences between the conversations 18 month olds had with their mothers and those of 30 month olds and their mothers.

As children moved from infancy through toddlerhood (18 to 36 months), mothers and children began to refer more frequently to the past, both to distant as well as recent nonpres-ent experiences. As children got older, they also included more detail in their descriptions of nonpresent events. While the par-ent of a 19 month old typically mentioned one key item from a past experience ("Did you have fun at Grandmother's last weekend?"), the parent of a 24 month old was more likely to embellish the core item with several details ("Did you have fun at Grandmother's last weekend, when we jumped in the leaves and we petted the pony, Thumbelina?").

Between the second and third birthdays, children and their parents were more likely to use a truly conversational format to discuss the past, and their conversations also became longer. While the mother of a 19 month old was likely to do almost all of the talking when the past was discussed, a 24 month old and her mother might take turns asking and telling about a previous experience. For many pairs, the older the child, the more turns are taken in a given conversation about the past. The partners used their turns to trade information, to keep the conversation going, to ask for information from each other, and to express interest or acknowledge the other person's contribution.

Not all of the mothers and children talked about the past in the same way. Among the most striking aspects of these conversations were the differences in the way individual mother-child pairs referred to the past and used these refer-ences. The couples seemed to fall into two clear groups, one group that loved to talk about the past for its own sake, which we called reminiscing, and one group that seemed to refer to the past quickly for purposes of clarification and utility, which we called practical remembering pairs.

Identifying Collaboration

One of the most compelling aspects of these data was that mothers and their children seemed to be a collaborative team, co-constructing an account of their past. But the questions remain: What is the best way to identify stories that are told across speakers? How should we characterize the nature of this interaction? In this study we identified collaboration by extracting all episodes of talk about the past in which there was more than one statement and response (question and answer, description and addition by the other speaker, and so on). These episodes of talk had to contain relevant consecutive contributions to the narrative by both mother and child. That is, the parent and child had to speak for more than two turns and had to stay on the topic, describing an experience or event, as in this example:

Charlotte: *(age 22 1/2 months)* Boo boo.
Mother: Where's your boo boo? Let me see. *(Charlotte shows her mother the bruise on her hand)*
Mother: You have a boo boo? Where? Oh, yes. Who did that boo boo? Mommy did that boo boo. Mommy did that boo boo, didn't she? Did mommy do that boo boo to you?
Charlotte: Yeah.
Mother: What'd she do? She caught your finger in that step-stool, huh?
Charlotte: *(touches her thumb)* Bunny.
Mother: Yes, it hurt, didn't it?
Charlotte: Bunny.
Mother: Yes, and I put a Band-Aid on it, remember?
Charlotte: Oh.
Mother: Remember? We showed the doctor last week and he said the nail was coming in just fine. Mother thought she had ruined your manicures for life. *(Charlotte bangs cymbals)*
Mother: Those your cymbals?

To see the co-constructed narrative, we can order the elements into a complete story, including contributions by both participants:

> Charlotte has a boo boo.
>
> Mother gave it to her.
>
> Mother caught Charlotte's finger in a stepstool. It hurt.
>
> Mother put a Band-Aid on it.
>
> The doctor saw it last week.
>
> He said it was getting better.

To see what parent and child each contribute to the story, and to track changes over time in the nature of their contributions to the overall account of the event, the next step is to allot responsibility to each participant for the various components of the total narrative.

Charlotte initiated this conversation, but it was not clear whether she meant to frame it in terms of a past event. Temporal framing at this early age is usually the mother's job ("Who did that boo boo?"). The mother supplied this information, although only after trying unsuccessfully to get Charlotte to supply it. After the mother elaborates on the origins of the cut, Charlotte seems to have taken in enough of her mother's description to add something to it ("Bunny"). This addition causes her mother to add something that is relevant, but probably is not what Charlotte intended ("Yes, it hurt, didn't it?"). Charlotte persists with her contribution, although she is dependent on her mother to turn it into a coherent part of the narrative ("Yes, and I put a Band-Aid on it, remember?"). The mother asks if Charlotte remembers that element of the event, even though Charlotte brought it into the narrative. Finally, the mother uses Charlotte's emphasis 'on the Band-Aid to introduce another relevant element of her daughter's past experience, the visit to the doctor. Here we can see that Charlotte plays an important role in directing the narrative (she initiates the topic, focuses on the Band-Aid, mention of which eventually leads to the inclusion of the reference to the doctor's visit). But the mother is responsible for framing the conversation, for making the connections between the items, and for maintaining the sequence of events both within the dialogue and as they originally happened.

Developmental Shifts in Co-Construction

◆

For the 18- to 19-month-old children in these interactions, the mother was the central and predominant constructor of the narrative. To the extent that the child showed interest or offered verbal acknowledgment of what the mother was referring to, she was trying to be part of the reminiscing activity and a partner to the narrative, although not actually contributing substance to it.

Mother: Susan's writing—we write, too.
Charlotte: *(age 19 months)* Points in her mouth while looking at her mother.
Mother: That's right—and yesterday you put it in your mouth. *(Referring to a crayon Charlotte uses to draw and had tried to eat the day before)*

In this example the child is completely dependent on the mother to turn her gesture into a comment about a past action. Her mother creates the topical frame in which Charlotte can refer to the writing. Finally, the mother's discussion is framed as past talk because the child refers to something about writing that is specific and that happened in the past. Neither one would have referred to this particular action without the other participant, and neither one contributes a full statement about the past.

Mother: (*while looking at a doll clown with her 19-month-old-daughter*) You looked like this. Remember, the other day we dressed you up like this? Huh? Where'd you go? You went to a party? You went to a Halloween party. (*Christa is only partially attentive to her mother's narrative.*) Remember? I put pom-poms on your dress?
Christa: Pom-pom.
Mother: Pom-poms. And d'you remember what you got at the party?
Christa: Pom-pom.
Mother: You got pom-poms, yeah. We fixed your pom-poms up when we came home. And what else did you get? A balloon?
Christa: Balloon.
Mother: And the pumpkin.
Christa: Pumpkin, pumpkin, pumpkin.
Mother: (*pointing to a pumpkin on the table*) There he is.
Christa: Pumpkin.

Christa's mother frames the discussion in terms of the past from the outset by setting the scene, using the past tense, naming a time, and asking: "Remember?" Mention of pom-

poms obviously attracts Christa's attention, and when she sticks with it, her mother switches momentarily to that focus, elaborating on it ("Yeah. We fixed your pom-poms up when we came home."). By incorporating the child's interest, she also sequences that piece of the story, and thus it becomes part of a narrative.

This child does not contribute any new information, but she participates in the narrative by repeating some of her mother's words. Much of their dialogue is participatory rather than contributory. This suggests that they are at a stage of joint attention to the past rather than jointly reconstructing the past through narrative. Such early noninformative contributions of children appear to be efforts to show they are interested in what their mothers are talking about. At the same time, mothers who talk about the past in an engaging way before their children are really ready to contribute information may be trying to interest their children in considering continuities in their experiences. A description of a past episode can be thought of as a kind of mental object. Early interaction often seems to involve trying to coordinate attention to that mental object. In the process children begin to learn that descriptions of the past are a distinct kind of talk.

In those pairs where co-construction was not apparent, the mother's style of introducing a topic from the past and of querying her child about a remembered event differed from that in the co-constructing pairs. Often these mothers did little stage setting and began by asking direct questions about an event that were not sufficient to create co-construction or even interest the child. This is evident here:

The mother of a 19 month old to her daughter:

Mother: So, Lisa, what did you do this morning with Andrew and Emily?

Lisa: Yaya.
Mother: Ya ya?
Lisa: Yayayaya.
Mother: Had a nice time, heh? Did you look at pictures of
the kitties? And did you do the puzzle? Lisa, can you say
"Susie"?

During this conversation, Lisa is rocking in her rocking chair, while her mother is sitting behind her on a couch. The mother and child do not share a joint focus on each other, just as they don't share a joint focus on the object of conversation. The mother's questions are unrelated to one another and thus do not offer Lisa an interesting, clear, or developed description of the event. The mother expects her child to articulate internalized knowledge about the past, but has failed to create a narrative scene that the child can enter or to which she can easily attend.

Co-Construction in 24 Month Olds

◆

In the 24-month-age group co-constructions contained more differentiated roles for mother and child. The child had developed an increasingly internalized construction of her past, which allowed her to contribute meaningful information to a dialogue from her own point of view. Even when the child at this age can contribute new information to the narrative, however, it is still cooperatively remembered. Without the mother's framing questions and supportive interpretations, the child's pieces of information would have no sequence, temporal perspective, or explicit meaning within the current context.

This next example demonstrates how a pair at this stage make a past event into a story that can be repeated. Faith, who has just had her second birthday, appropriates more and more of the narrative. As the story is repeated, the roles shift slightly. But even in the first telling, Faith contributes by keeping the mother going, using the temporal connective "then."

Faith and her mother are in the kitchen talking about a toy called a Snork:

Mother: I'm trying to think back about Snork. We got Snork at the toy store, remember? We went to the toy store and we saw a great big Snork—at the toy store.

Faith: See it?

Mother: You don't remember?

Faith: See a great big Snork?

Mother: I have to tell you about it. It was a long time ago. Faith and Mommy and Daddy all went to the toy store and we saw a big, big Snork.

Faith: A little Snork?

Mother: And there was a little, little Snork. And remember what the big Snork was doing? The big Snork was waving at Faith.

Faith: Then?

Mother: And the little Snork—you know what the little Snork did?

Faith: Hm?

Mother: The little Snork talked to Daddy and said, "I wanna go with Faith."

Faith: Then?

Mother: And so when we left the toy store, after we had looked at all the toys, we left the toy store—Daddy looked in his pocket and saw Snork was there! And he gave it to Faith.

Faith: Again.

Mother: One day Faith and Mommy and Daddy all went . . . to . . . the . . . grocery store?

Faith: Toy store!

Mother: Toy store! And what did we see?

Faith: A big Snork and a little Snork and a big, big one and a little, little Big Bird.

Mother: Oh! What were the big Snork and Big Bird doing? (Faith and her mother play word games on big and little.)

Mother: Little Snork. Remember what the little Snork did? What did that little Snork do?

Faith: Talk at—talk to . . . talk to . . . Mom have some more coffee.

Mother: No, thanks. I'm drinking juice, actually.

Faith: Mommy tell story about toy store.

Mother: Okay, one day Faith and Mommy and Daddy all went to the toy store and when we got there we saw a big Snork and the Snork was waving at you. There was a big Snork and there was a little Snork.

Faith: Snork talk to Daddy.

Mother: Yeah and what did that little Snork say?

Faith: (in a Snork voice) I want to go to . . . I want to go to . . .

Mother: Mm, so what happened after we came out of the toy store? (Faith wants to play with water and they switch to a discussion of water play.)

To introduce the narrative this mother begins with a central theme, "getting Snork at a toy store," and immediately tags it as a memory ("Remember?"). The child shows interest but does not seem to understand that a past experience is being recounted. The mother stresses the remembering aspect of the narrative ("You don't remember? It was a long time ago").

After the mother then sets the narrative stage, Faith can contribute some appropriate information ("A little Snork"). The mother continues to sequence and embellish. The child keeps the narrative going ("Then?") and shows her increasing mastery of the narrative. She also wants to practice the story ("Again, Mommy tell story about toy store").

In contrast, the mother of Zachary, who has just celebrated his second birthday, does not set the stage for her child's contribution but, rather, sticks to a simple formula:

Mother: Did you tell Susan about your party?
Zachary: Party.
Mother: Did you have a party?
Zachary: Yeah.
Mother: What song did they sing for you?
Zachary: Happy Birthday.
Mother: Yeah, how old were you at your party?
Zachary: Mmmmm.
Mother: How old?
Zachary: Two.
Mother: Two?
Zachary: Yeah.
Mother: Were your friends there?
Zachary: Yeah.
Mother: Who was at your party?
Zachary: Pat.
Mother: Who? Pat? Who else?
Zachary: Lea.
Mother: Lea. Who else?
Zachary: Bobby.
Mother: Bobby and who else?
Zachary: Lea.
Mother: Lea and who else?

Zachary: Pa.
Mother: Papa and who else?
Zachary: Lea.
Mother: *Who else?*
Zachary: Papa.
Mother: Who else was there?
Zachary: Lea.
Mother: Were any of your friends there?
Zachary: Yeah.
Mother: Who?
Zachary: Zachary.
Mother: Zachary and who else?
Zachary: Papa.

Rather than weaving her child's responses into a narrative, this mother simply continues to try to elicit information. When her questions do not produce the answers she seeks, she persists anyway. In response, the child begins to repeat the same information over and over again. Very little about the birthday party ends up being described; there is no sequencing and little detail. Although the child engages very successfully in the question-answer format, there is minimal co-construction of the past event.

Co-Construction in 30 Month Olds

◆

In the 30-month-old group co-construction looked somewhat different than it did in the earlier age groups. In couples with successful co-construction, the child was a more active participant. The mother used less prodding and framing and more direct questioning. The child often added information that the mother did not already have and typically used the past tense correctly.

Molly, who is just over 30 months of age, and her mother are discussing the child's first night in her new bed. Molly's representation of the event seems to have crystallized sufficiently to allow her to give information about it to her mother. Yet her mother's question leads to information that Molly might not have included in her representation on her own.

Molly: And where did you put it (the blanket)?
Mother: Well, I put it in the closet because I—Molly slept in her bed last night.
Molly: No and I fall down.
Mother: She rolled off—and you—did you—when did you roll off that bed?
Molly: I just—inside I just sleep on-on—on the carpet.
Mother: But did you roll off that bed in the middle of the night or in the morning?
Molly: In-in-in inside the middle of the night.
Mother: You did? Why didn't you call me? I would have come down and put you back up there. You should've called me. Did it hurt?
Molly: No it didn't hurt.
Mother: Oh great.
Molly: I know, but I slept inside the floor with my brother and me.

Besides the sophistication of this couple's ability to discuss the past, it is interesting to note Molly's attempt to place the fall in time, at her mother's request. This represents a new level of maternal demands and a new set of skills the child must tackle in her attempt to reminisce like an adult. In addition to achieving a new level of cooperative remembering, this child, like a number of children her age, adds fantasy material to her narrative; she in fact does not have a brother. This tendency of older children to incorporate fantasy material into their autobiographical narratives suggests that by the time they are 30 months old they have internalized a concept of the past as story material in which all kinds of information can be integrated.

To go back to the earlier question of the interweaving of fact and fantasy, Molly and her mother's conversation illustrates that in its earliest manifestation, merging fact and fantasy is a sign that the 3 year old is organizing all kinds of experience into a narrative framework. Separating those two domains of experience into two types of stories will come later in development.

In general, 30-month-old children and their mothers were more likely to pick out an act or segment from an overall event and describe it in detail, mentioning time, place, and feelings rather than listing scattered aspects of the event. This may reflect the child's increased ability to maintain a focus on a particular act or event without the support of a broad description. In fact, one way to characterize the early development of narratives is as a transition from broad and shallow accounts to ones that are more circumscribed but deeper.

Early mother-child discourse about the past can be seen as a kind of collaboration in which each participant contributes in coordination with the other. The balance and responsibilities of the partnership change with the child's age. At first, mother and child engage in a shared activity in which the child has a somewhat undifferentiated role. Coordination in this early phase involves joint attention to the past. Over time the coordination manifests itself through verbal dialogues in which both partners help construct a narrative about a past experience. Some conversations reveal a mutually agreed-upon version of the past, whereas in others, particularly with older children, a version of the past is negotiated by the pair.

Individual Differences in Co-Construction

❖

Co-construction seemed to primarily occur in couples where the mother emphasized reminiscing as an important interesting activity. In other words, sharing a narrative and co-constructing an event from the past usually occurred where there was a mother who focused on past talk for its own sake. It is not surprising to find that a child can only do his or her part in the joint effort if he or she has a mother who is willing to establish the stage in which the cooperative work can take place.

Reminiscing pairs referred to the past often and at length. Their descriptions usually included considerable detail and several conversational turns. Most striking, however, was that their recollections of past experiences seemed to serve a purpose in and of itself. It is as if they were saying, "Let's talk about the past, let's reminisce together." This comes through vividly when Charlotte and her mother discuss her cut, or Faith and her mother discuss Snork.

The format that reminiscing mothers used to refer to the past followed a pattern that seemed developmentally geared to the child's changing ability. When Charlotte was between 19 and 21 months old, her mother's style was dominated by the monologue or reporting format. By the time Charlotte was 22 months, the mother's references were dominated by requests for acknowledgments and yes/no questions, and by the time Charlotte celebrated her second birthday, the mother's conversations contained more requests for specific information.

Practical remembering pairs, in contrast, seemed to talk about the past primarily in the service of some ongoing activity. In effect, the message to the child is: The past is useful for clarifying or adding to the present. As one mother said to her child, "Here, you put the puzzle piece here. Remember how I showed you yesterday?" Compared to reminiscing pairs, practical remembering pairs referred to past experiences less frequently. Their discussions involved fewer turns, and their descriptions were briefer and less detailed.

Does this stylistic difference in the why and how of talking about the past have any significance for children's development of a narrative sense, or does it all come out in the wash? One of the more interesting findings of this study was that in analyses of the final tapes of the four couples studied over a six-month period, and in analyses of the child's contributions within the eighteen mother-child pairs recorded only once, children in the reminiscing pairs were more able to independently contribute information in conversations as they passed their second birthday than children in the practical remembering pairs. These results suggest that when mothers and children engage in talking about the past in an enriched way, and in families where talking about the past is a valued activity in its own right, toddlers show an enhanced ability and proclivity to contribute independent information to these conversations.

This conclusion regarding the consistent relationship between cooperative rememberers and a rich, embellished frequent style of memory talk suggests that intersubjectivity or shared remembering works as a powerful device for helping the child internalize forms of memory talk. In couples where memory talk is not the site of development, cooperation is not apparent, although it perhaps could be found in alternative forms of talk and interaction.

Do these differences in style of talking about the past persist beyond toddlerhood? We recorded stories children tell one another in day care. Some of these preschoolers, ranging in age from 3 to 5 years, employ the reminiscing style, and others use the practical remembering style when telling about past experiences. We have not seen these preschoolers with their parents, so we cannot say for sure whether the children's style of talking about the past with friends always corresponds to the style they use at home when talking with their parents. But our observations do suggest that the two styles we have identified are a pervasive and useful way of characterizing how children differ from one another in the way they talk about the past. For instance, some recent research seems to show that shy preschoolers are more likely to use the practical remembering style and outgoing children are more likely to use the reminiscing style.

Learning to Tell the Right Kind of Story

◆

Children learn to tell stories about personal experience in the context of social interaction, particularly with parents and perhaps with other family members. As we've seen, such social interaction is not only the context for early storytelling, it also appears to be a primary means by which children become storytellers. One of the strengths of this view of the developmental process is that it helps to explain how children learn to tell stories that are valued by their particular community.

Research on the collaborative nature of early talk about the past suggests that children have the chance to internalize family styles of narrative right from the beginning. Children constantly hear stories being told. Sometimes parents tell them stories; at other times they hear parents, other adults, and siblings tell each other stories.

In the first two or three years of a child's life, the parent has an enormous investment in collaborating with him, helping him along in the ways of talking. Catherine Snow has pointed out that this is not simply because parents want to be good teachers. More selfishly, it is because they are talking to their potential future conversational partner. Getting your child to become an able conversationalist will have a payoff—someone you can talk to!

But after a child has become fairly adept (able to communicate wishes and needs, able to understand instructions), the nature of language between parent and child shifts from a tutorial or master-apprentice one to a looser, less focused interaction. Children of 3 to 7 years are more on their own and may have to work harder to get the attention of the adults in their lives. Among other skills, they need to be good at telling the right kind of story. The same goes for school life, which begins, for most children, some time between 3 and 5 years of age.

So, for instance, kids have to learn how to begin their stories.

Do they start with "Once upon a time" or "Do you know what happened to me?" or do they just jump in with an opening line such as "George found a girlfriend at the mall"? Children need to learn *when* to tell a story, *what* to put in it, and *how* best to tell it. Should they stick to the simplest story line possible, or should they tell elaborate and complex versions? Should the moral of the story determine what gets told, or should some standard of accuracy or keeping the interest of the listener be of primary importance?

Children themselves often provide implicit and explicit feedback to one another about what makes a story good, what would make a story better, and what they most want to hear about. This happens implicitly through the questions they ask about, and additions they make to one another's accounts:

Jack: I went to the movies last night with my baby-sitter.
Henry: Was it scary?
Jack: Yeah, it was REAL scary.
Henry: Well, like, like did it have a dracula or a murder or something in it?

Henry, through his questions, is letting Jack know what would be exciting to hear about the movie. Alison Preece has shown that children act as explicit critics of one another, commenting, for example, on the truthfulness or likelihood of something reported in a story. Preschool children thus seem to do for one another some of the things parents do for younger storytellers.

As children venture out into school and the larger community, they may also begin to encounter new criteria for what constitutes a good story. In a study of two neighboring southern communities, Roadville and Trackton (discussed in Chapter 2), Shirley Brice Heath describes how both groups of children, when they get to school, encounter a different set of criteria and expectations regarding what constitutes a story.

When the first-grade teacher says in introducing a social studies unit on community helpers, "now we all know some story about the job of the policeman," she conjures up for the children different images of policemen and stories about them, but the concept of story which holds in this school context is one which refers to factual narratives of events in which policemen are habitually engaged. Following their home model, Roadville children might conceive of such a story as "telling on" a policeman or recounting his failure to follow certain rules. Trackton children would expect stories of a policeman to exaggerate the facts and to entertain with witticisms and verbal play.

The children themselves in these communities are aware of the different standards adults have for stories. Two little Roadville girls, about 7 years old, have been telling stories on the bus ride home:

Sally: That story, you just told, you know that ain't so.
Wendy: I'm not tellin' no story, uh-er-ah, no I'm tellin' the kind Miss Wash *[her teacher]* talks about.
Sally: Mamma won't let you get away with that kinda excuse. You know better.
Wendy: What are you so, uh excited about? We got one kinda story mamma knows about, and a whole 'nother one we do at school. They're different *// looking at Sally //* and you know it=
Sally: You better hope mamma knows it, if she catches you making up stuff like that.

The development of storytelling does not end with the preschool age, but it is during the first three years that the crucial seeds of talk about the past and the narrative form blossom. It is during this early phase that children learn what it is to refer to the past, and they internalize parental and community values about when, why, and how they should tell stories.

Between the ages of 5 and 10, children typically acquire the ability to sequence clearly and, if needed, accurately, describe events in a logical way that conveys cause and effect, diverge from a plot in order to add explanation or detail, and then return to the main plot and include explicit authorial commentary in their stories. Many of these aspects of narrative development appear under almost all typical conditions, as a function of general cognitive and linguistic development. That is, children in general become more logical, learn about the relationship between cause and effect, become more aware of the need to tell about an event as it really happened, and discern more of the potential differences between an "objective" account of an event and their interpretations of the event.

After the age of 3, what is less well known is why and how some children have come to love to tell stories, whereas other children steadily lose both interest and confidence in telling stories. Typically, most children can, under the right circumstances, achieve all of the things necessary to put together a correct if boring story, but fewer and fewer children seem to engage in storytelling as a central way of communicating personal experience and ideas.

6

♦

Developing a Narrative Voice

♦

> *My grandma is 85 and as harsh as a beehive*
> *and my mother is*
> *a hostile exile.*
>
> *I would rather bother with*
> *my father but he's hardly*
> *ever around.*
>
> *My brothers and sister*
> *are bruises all on the family body.*
>
> *My cat is a whole different thing*
> *he has no bites or sting*
> *So when things go*
> *wrong and he's oh so strong*
> *I always go to my cat*
> *cause he knows where it's at.*

My mother is very pretty. I would like to kiss her and hug her. When I am at school I miss her.

Both these pieces were written by 9-year-old children. Both are about family members, and both were written at the request of a teacher. But there the similarities end. The first is passionate and idiosyncratic, the second sparse and more conventional. The first has a strong personal voice to it, a particular rhythm and imagery that match the feelings conveyed, whereas the second could have been written by any number of children.

Writing teachers and psychologists have generated two streams of literature about children's storytelling that rarely intersect, even though they share certain concerns and interests. Educators have been promoting the virtues of open-ended as opposed to highly prescribed writing, free-form exercises as opposed to formulaic writing assignments. The teacher who might once have insisted that students write poems that rhyme or tell stories that begin with "Once upon a time" now encourages children to write in a journal about whatever they want and in a style that suits them.

By the same token, whereas once a teacher would have been urged to correct bad grammar, or to tell the child to add four more sentences, now many teachers are encouraged to accept, even praise whatever the child comes up with and to tolerate a wide range of formats. One distinction often lost in this generally positive shift in educational practice is that between open-ended activities and aesthetic development. The two are related but not synonymous. Giving children license to write whatever they want fosters creativity. But aesthetic development requires immersion in activities and materials that are dense with aesthetic qualities. It involves joint attention by the adult and child to beauty and meaning.

The second stream of literature comes from cognitive and developmental psychologists interested in how children's stories give us access to the way in which children organize information and experience. The investigators tend to focus almost exclusively on how stories are structured; they pay little attention to the kind of irreverent language, quirky imagery, and personal expression that many writing teachers value. Such subtleties, variations of tone, choice of words, emphases and omissions, however, are very important in children's narratives, both aesthetically and in terms of what a child's story means, what it tells us.

The power of language to tell us about our lives lies in its nuances. This is what the novelist George Eliot meant when deploring antiseptic and conventional use of language in storytelling:

> A language which has no uncertainty, no whims of idiom, no cumbrous forms, no fitful shimmer of many-hued significance, no hoary archaisms "familiar with forgotten years" [is] a patent deodorized and non-resonant language which effects the purpose of communication as perfectly and rapidly as algebraic signs. Your language may be a perfect medium of expression to science, but will never express LIFE, which is a great deal more than science.

When writing teachers encourage open-ended assignments, their reason for doing so tends to be simply that this makes the process more joyous for children or that it leads eventually to better quality writing or both. The long-term psychological and narrative effect of using this kind of expression receives less serious attention. But in the opening examples of writing by two 9 year olds, the first piece is not only more interesting to read, more lively, and filled with more vivid images and information, the writer seems to express who he is and how he feels much more clearly and strongly than the second child. He is more able to construct a particular meaning and to communicate that meaning. And that is bound to have an impact on him psychologically, both in the immediate situation in which he constructs and communicates his narrative and also in the long-term developmental process of self-reflection and the sharing of those reflections with others. The kind of writing in this poem doesn't just happen, particularly not by the time children are as entrenched in conventional school ways as most 9 year olds are.

On the wall of a second-grade classroom I visited, each child had hung a silhouette of him- or herself. Above this they had pasted a collage of pictures from magazines that they felt expressed who they were. Below each silhouette the child had put a self-description in the form of a riddle. The idea was that a parent would enter the room on visiting night and be able to guess which profile/poem was his or her child's. The riddles, for the most part, went something like this: "My eyes are blue / My hair is brown / I like strawberry ice cream / Who am I?" or "I have freckles / I live by the lake / I love to play basketball / Who am I?" Among these was one that read "I'm a yapper / My name is Captain Zinc / I'm cute / Guess who?" Why does one child use language in a more original and expressive way, when all the children are in the same class and were assigned the same project? One child has his own narrative voice, and its distinctiveness is loud and clear. How did it get to be that way?

A child is choosing between different-colored candies. She leans toward them and says: "Give me the rrrude, rrrrippppy, rrrreddd one." She might have just said, "Give me the red one." But she didn't. She makes her request more than a simple or transparent transaction. She makes it an expression of herself and her experience of reality as well as a tool for fulfilling a transaction.

In Chapter 5 I talked about the origins of storytelling: how and when it begins, how it grows, and what role parents play in the development of the narrative process. Children, early on, get different messages about what makes a good story, and they are often amazingly receptive to those messages. Not only do children learn when to tell a story, and what kind of story to tell, they also learn how to tell a story. Part of the "how" comes from shared cultural values and habits (such as the kind described by Shirley Brice Heath). But some aspects are more personally distinctive and arise from the individual experiences of the child, what stories he is exposed to, and what he is encouraged to make of them.

What Is Narrative Voice?

Narrative voice refers to the notion that every story is expressed through a person and through that person's use of a medium, language. The person speaking and the language he uses shape, color, and highlight the events and ideas being described. The style and genre in which he tells his story express who he is as an individual as well as how he fits into his culture. Psychological processes are expressed through a communicative medium, according to the influential Russian literary theorist Mikhail Bakhtin. And the medium through which they are expressed in turn shapes the psychological processes and their products. Scholars of Bakhtin's work have referred to this notion as "the speaking personality, the speaking consciousness."

You can ask of any narrative: Who is telling the story? What is his relationship to the events described? How does he feel about the events? In some books, like *David Copperfield*, the apparent storyteller is also the protagonist. The question in a story like that always is, Where is the author in the book? Is the voice of Dickens the same as Copperfield's? In other books, where the narrator keeps a lower profile and appears more objective, as in Jane Austen's novels, the narrator's personality and view come across through tone, imagery, and often simply the apparent meaning of the events described. You can forget for pages at a time that there is an author who is controlling the description; then some twist of events or language can remind you suddenly that this is someone's fiction rather than a set of objective events. So one question about narrative voice always is: Who is telling the story? This leads to a second question: What are the qualities of that voice? What qualities of language, rhythm, and sensibility, in other words, are conveyed through the telling of the story?

In psychology, the concept of voice is a powerful though neglected one. Used in a psychological sense, narrative voice is a metaphor that refers to the medium that conveys experience and ideas. But it shares some characteristics of "voice" used in the physical sense—the sounds produced by our vocal cords. Like a physical voice, it has some characteristics one has no control over (if you are a woman your voice may be at a higher pitch than a man's). Some aspects of your voice reflect experience and environment in ways that are not under immediate or flexible control (if you've smoked you have a husky voice, if you've been running your voice will sound breathy, and so forth). And some aspects of voice may be products of the moment, and may or may not be under your control. You can usually but not always keep your voice calm, you can inflect it, raise it, soften your pronunciation.

The same holds true for the telling of a story. Some characteristics of how you tell a story are the result of things over which you have little direct control—your gender and age-related experiences, often your deepest cultural assumptions.

Some characteristics of how you tell a story are the result of your personal life experiences with telling stories—whether you were given practice in a variety of narrative forms and encouraged to tell stories in your own way, whether you were corrected a lot and taught to answer very specific questions about your past experiences, whether you were applauded for making up words and using words in new ways. And some aspects of how you tell a story are influenced by the immediate situation: Are you asked to talk about something that interests you? Do you have a receptive audience? How was the storytelling initiated? What other stories have been told?

The narrative voice consists of the distinctive set of characteristics that make up the way in which a story is told. The same content can be told in many different ways and thus take on quite different meanings. It is through narrative voice that one attains a sense of the distinctiveness of one's story, and it is through an authentic narrative voice that one can really express oneself. This is perhaps why children who are educated in a nonnative language are often at such a disadvantage. Not only are they likely to have difficulty with such everyday literacy tasks as following instructions in a textbook, they may be unable to express their deepest feelings and conceptions of themselves in a second language.

For our purposes, an authentic narrative voice tells the story in a way that is consistent with who is doing the telling and what is intended by the tale. With children this means that their tone, their perspective, what they focus on, and how they express experience are true to who they believe themselves to be.

Some kinds of stories and storytelling situations lend themselves more than others to the force or distinctiveness of personal voice. For instance, if you are in court recounting what you remember of a traffic accident you witnessed, there is little call or tolerance for the idiosyncrasies of a personal narrative voice. In court testimony, language is supposed to be transparent; presenting information in its most stable objective form is essential. The filter of a distinctive voice, the interpretation of an experience through one's personal thoughts, feelings, and perceptions is a hindrance, not an object of interest. On the other hand, one's memoirs are only interesting insofar as they are conveyed through a personal voice.

Where do the narratives of children fit into this schema of distinctiveness? Most children begin their narrative careers with a rich sense of personal voice. As suggested in the discussion of children's autobiographies, the close relationship between early language and experience allows children to convey what they have experienced with unusual directness. The fact that young storytellers are smack in the middle of a love affair with this powerful new world of words means that, if encouraged in the slightest, they will relish the words they use and be eager to experiment with new ones. It is easy for an adult to forget how intoxicating it is for the young child to discover that everything has a name, that words can be put together in almost infinite combinations to mean new things, that you can get things done with words, that you can say how you feel with words, that you can affect the way others feel, that you are much more of a presence in a room of others if you too can use words. No wonder young language learners look so gleeful and triumphant as they announce, "That's a big dog!" "I want more milk," "Toilet face, toilet face, toilet face," and so on.

Children often express their communicative enthusiasm with their bodies as well as with words. As Claudia Lewis has pointed out, "Piaget has said that to silence a child's tongue is to silence his thinking. We might add: to immobilize his body is to silence his language and his thought." Lewis describes the way children often jump up at circle time and say their poem or story accompanied by body movements, large and small. David MacNeil approaches this phenomenon from a different perspective. He shows how children often use gesture to convey a second level of text that is not embodied in the spoken words. This fusion of bodily sensation and word meaning gives the child an artist's potential power with language, and it carries over to an obvious sensual pleasure in words themselves. Young children delight in the connections between form and meaning, sound and sense, which is why they rhyme, alliterate, use puns, and make up words, why they say rrrrrude rrrrippppy rrrreddd instead of red.

After a trip to Orlando, the 4-year-old son of some friends insisted that they refer to Disney World as Gaga doo Gaga. Recently the same child announced to his teachers that everyone was either ka dee dee or kadoodoo. He went on to explain that it had something to do with the hair on your head and added, by way of illumination, "In winter the trees are kadeedee, but in summer they are kadoo doo." The words are silly, made up; but they show that this 4 year old feels that language is malleable, expressive, and fun. It is his to use.

The natural expressiveness, or voice, of the very young child by itself is not enough. To flower, it has to be given form, and that's where aesthetics (style, genre, and the like) come in. Unfortunately, in the process of learning about form, some of the vibrancy of the young child's language use is often lost. In looking at the differences among the personal memories of, say, 4, 7, and 9 year olds, two things become apparent. Many children become better testifiers and they become worse storytellers. That is, their stories become longer, more sequential, more detailed and coherent, but also often less interesting and less personal. Often in these recountings of personal memories, one learns less about the storyteller and more about the event in the narratives of older schoolchildren. Consider, for example, these two personal memories, the first written by a 5 year old, the second by a 9 year old.

> *My best memory is a tropical fish. I caught it at a lake. We ate it. I caught it with a worm. It tasted good.*

> *I remember we were going to get a deck on our house. Soon the carpenters came with the wood. First they had to cut down the wall and put the sliding glass door in. The next day they started digging four big holes. They were five feet deep. Next they put big posts in the holes and cemented them in. The next day they started putting the deck floor together. The boards were put together. Like a zigzag. It's called haringbone (sic). Soon it was finished. It was a pretty deck.*

These two stories exemplify differences in the narratives of these two age groups in American culture. The differences signal development of some kind. As children get older, they gain the ability to order descriptive sentences so that the description matches the order of actions and elements within the event; they become more able to accurately depict an event, describe things so that they make sense, and open and close a description in a way that lets the reader know it is beginning and ending. But the differences also suggest certain losses in the way older children tell stories. The second narrative is drier; its relative completeness carries with it a kind of deadness as a description. The first is livelier and more expressive of the experiencing self. How should we characterize the change in storytelling that seems to occur with age?

Development is not synonymous with change or even maturation but involves reorganization of processes and behavior that follow certain paths or sequences and that lead to a qualitative difference in the process and its products. Psychologists view any given set of changes or reorganizations as part of a developmental process if they lead toward some identified end state, or telos, that reflects the stages or levels leading up to it.

The telos we define for narrative has an important effect on what we see as the developmental path of narrative processes in children. The implicit telos of storytelling traditionally used by most developmental researchers is the ability to recount events accurately and completely and portray events in a logical way that clearly identifies a problem or dramatic high point. This telos leads researchers and others to look at young children's narratives in terms of those abilities. Young children seem to lack those abilities and gain them as they get older. It happens that these are also the characteristics encouraged in our school system.

If we define the telos, or ideal end state, of the development of storytelling as the ability to tell stories that describe and evoke experience in the reader, however, the path of narrative development looks different. With this different telos in mind, such characteristics of young children's narratives as vividness signal early glimmers of fully developed storytelling that will remain only that if they are not nurtured in the culture. The environments in which children grow up expand some aspects of storytelling and shrink others.

What types of social and educational processes influence the development and use of a child's personal narrative voice? The two most important seem to be the type of response a child encounters from her listeners and the stories she is exposed to. We can see the effects of each of these in small time scales, but unfortunately while we can make plausible arguments about the long-term effects, no one has carefully investigated these; indeed, it would be very difficult to do so.

How Feedback Shapes the Narrative Voice

◆

As described in Chapter 4, when children are very young they are more likely to tell stories with their parents than to their parents. What the parent says and asks shapes the child's verbal account of the past. As children get older, they can construct their private memories and stories in words more independently of the adult. But the adult as audience can still have a large effect on the child's story. What the adult offers as verbal and nonverbal feedback can encourage or discourage the shaping of the story in certain directions and the development of certain of its characteristics.

A 3 year old is telling her father about an event she remembers from long before:

Child: We went up a mountain. And we saw a wolf!
Father: Really, a wolf? I don't think so. There are no wolves around here. Are you sure you saw a wolf?
Child: Oh, yes. A big, huge wolf. And he was grayish and blackish and reddish.
Father: You mean he was gray and black? He couldn't have been red. Wolves aren't red.

This father is attentive to the content of his child's story and shows through his questions that he values accuracy.

When he responds to her description, he not only questions it, but he changes the words, "grayish" to "gray," "blackish" to "black," and so forth. He is revising her story in the context of listening and showing interest, and in revising it he modifies her narrative voice.

Sometimes adults are eager to get more information or a specific type of information that they think children should be giving. This can redirect or halt the story the child might otherwise tell. Four-year-old Paul comes up to a girl in his day-care center: "Stephanie, guess what? I went to Nashville. Tennessee!!!! I saw Big Foot!!! I saw a real Big Foot. And it was this big *(holding out his hands)*." Stephanie doesn't respond immediately but shows interest in his story and remains engaged by standing close to him and looking at him. The teacher, however, says in a loud voice, "Paul. What else did you see in Nashville?" Paul doesn't answer, so the teacher repeats her question. At this point, Paul wanders off to join Stephanie, who had left when the teacher intervened.

There's no way to know what would have happened to this story if the teacher had not interrupted. What does seem apparent, however, is that the teacher was interested in getting Paul to talk about or list the other things he saw rather than elaborating on his description of Big Foot, which seems to be what captivated him. Her interception seems to have led to the end of the story, and to the end of the two children's interaction.

These two examples depict spontaneous interactions between interested adults and children whom they know. Researchers have examined the listener's effect on children's stories in more controlled settings, using researchers' confederates instead of parents or teachers. In a wonderful study, Anthony Pellegrini and Lee Galda looked at the effect of various experimenters' questions on a child's narrative responses. They began their study with the hypothesis that children and adults often approach the same task with differing interpretations. When an adult says, "Tell me about this whale" and points to a picture of a whale, for example, the child may interpret that as a request to tell about the picture rather than, as the adult might have hoped, using it as a launching pad for an imaginative account of the adventure of a whale.

Pellegrini and Galda had one researcher ask boys and girls to tell them stories. They were particularly interested in identifying the ways in which the adult and child, through their dialogue, came to share an understanding of what it meant to tell a story. They found that not only did the children differ in their initial level of sophistication and interpretation of the tasks but that the confederate (who did not know the real goal of the study) varied her questions in response to differences between her notion of the task and that particular child's notion of the task as manifested in the child's answers. For instance, when a child responded with a nonnarrative answer to a request to tell the researcher about some blocks, the adult was likely, in the beginning, to engage in a conversation at the child's level:

Experimenter: OK. Hilda what do we have here? Can you tell me a story about these things?
Hilda: Building with blocks. *(But not talking or looking at E)*
Experimenter: Can you tell me what you're doing?
Hilda: *(shakes her head no without looking at E)*
Experimenter: You're building a tower aren't you.
Hilda: Yes.

Experimenter: Let's play that you're a builder and I'm your
   helper.

In such situations the adult takes a strong lead in trying to
draw the child into her definition of the narrative task. As the
child gained confidence and the adult and child established a
mutual sphere of activity and play, the experimenter was likely
to begin asking more pointed, or demanding, narrative questions, which in turn influenced the nature of the resulting story.

In another example of the powerful effect of listener
responses on children's stories, Gillian McNamee instructed
teachers to read stories to 5- and 6-year-old schoolchildren and
then have the children act out the stories they had been told.
The children were highly motivated to dramatize their stories,
she discovered, and the social interaction that surrounded their
dramatizations (feedback in the form of audience response,
questions, and so forth) led to increased complexity and
richness in their retellings of the stories. Her point is that
narratives are first and foremost a communicative tool
for young children, manifested by their drive to dramatize the
stories. The social negotiation involved in these dramatizations
led to what McNamee calls intrapersonal narrative development—the process develops between children rather than
merely within children.

One night at the dinner table, two brothers, aged 5 and 7,
begin regaling their parents with their water-play adventure at
summer camp that day:

Sam: And then I walked over to the house, and I was just a
   little wet, and I pulled the rope on the bucket, and I didn't

know it but the bucket had turned, and tipped over and poured water all over Austen and John Henry . . .

Gavin: Let me tell this part, Sam, and then I'll let you tell your favorite part.

The boys were telling the story together as a team, negotiating their parts as they went along. But the most striking thing was how a question of the father's shifted the focus of the story.

When the children seemed to have run out of steam and finished their story, the father interjected, "And were the kids mad at you?" They answered in unison, "No." But the father's question started them off on the story again. This time, however, they embellished it, adding a few runs, hides, and bucket splashes they had left out in the first telling. In this second telling it turned out that one bucket had been filled with mud and had been poured all over one of the kids. "Were the counselors upset?" the father asked. Sam, the younger brother, answered, "No. I didn't get into trouble. That's what made it so much fun. I didn't even get in trouble. We poured water all over those guys and the teachers didn't get mad at me." The father's introduction of the question of consequences had prompted Sam to add another level to the meaning or feeling of the experience. It was no longer simply a story about having an exciting play fight with friends. The father's interest and attention, as the parental audience, had helped shape the original narrative into a story about what you can get away with.

Variations in parental style of feedback often reflect aspects of the particular parent-child relationship, the adult's implicit reasons for listening to the child's story, and the context in which the story is told. Carole Peterson and Allyssa McCabe, for example, looked at the relationship between different styles of parental input and the child's narrative construction among ten parent-toddler pairs. In the course of their research, they discovered a difference between what they called a "topic-expansion" style of parental input and a "confrontational expansion" style. Parents who helped children expand their topic tended to follow up the child's remarks with open-ended questions that picked up where the child's comment had left off:

Mother: And did you get sick at school, Harriet?
Harriet: Yeah.
Mother: What made you sick?
Harriet: I got *(unintelligible)* my pants fall, fall down.
Mother: You got wee-wees in your pants and you fell down. Is that what you said? And who looked after you when you got sick?
Harriet: Helen.
Mother: Helena did. Did Helena look after you when you were sick?
Harriet: Yeah.

In contrast, the parent who uses confrontational expansion style keeps correcting the child:

Mother: Where did you see them?
Paul: At the field.
Mother: *In* a field.
Paul: And they ate some hay.
Mother: And they ate some hay.
Paul: And they took the doggy and they cuddles in, to a doggy.

Mother: They cuddles in to a doggy.

Paul: And he was asleep in the field.

Mother: *When* the dog was asleep in the field.

Paul: And a real dog came.

Mother: Oh they didn't cuddle into a *real* dog did they. It was a *toy* dog.

The narrative the child is ultimately likely or able to produce is in part shaped by the kind of style the parent uses in response to his child. Each experience of storytelling a child has influences his constantly developing narrative voice.

Often, at least in American culture, adults respond to children's stories with questions about the story. But response styles vary from one cultural community to another. In mainstream American school culture the teacher is expected to respond to a child's story with acknowledgments or with questions seeking expansion and explanation. Often a teacher will listen to a child tell a story about something that happened at home, and respond either with something like, "Uh huh," "I see," "You did?" or, as did the teacher described earlier, with something like, "What else did you see?"

The implicit or unconscious stance of the teacher is that it is her job either to "allow" children to tell her stories or to extend what the child is doing. This extension is similar to the kind of scaffolding that Jerome Bruner points out mothers do with their children. Mothers do this to ward off boredom, as Bruner suggests, or as Catherine Snow points out, to help nurture their future conversational companion. Teachers, on the other hand, use this kind of response as a pedagogical tool to help children learn how to answer questions and offer more complete descriptions. This pattern is not universal, though. Among African-Americans studied by Sarah Michaels, for example, parents seldom asked questions to extend or clarify a story; they tended to respond instead with stories of their own. In doing so not only were they responding in kind, but for the young apprentice storyteller they were displaying ways of storytelling.

However useful this response style is in the community and family context, it can be problematic for children in a school setting where they get a different response. In the classroom Michaels studied, near Boston, there were black and white children from different neighborhoods and traditions. The mode of storytelling in the classroom was for the teacher to respond to a child's story with questions: "So, did you have a nice time on your birthday?" for example. But these questions threw the black children in the group off track. Michaels suggests that although these children knew their own stories, and the purpose and meaning of those stories, they didn't necessarily know how to answer the teacher's questions. As a result, their stories were not elaborated or developed within the group setting. In contrast, the white children were able to answer the teacher's questions, and because they could follow up in the way the teacher expected, their stories in turn were given greater play within the group.

The Art of Listening and Storytelling

So far I have been talking about the importance of the adult's style of verbal feedback as a shaping influence on children's stories and as an expression of interest and approval. But attentive listening in and of itself may also have a large impact on children's tendency to continue telling stories as they get older. As Gordon Wells has pointed out, the kind of extended stories that may be tolerated, even encouraged, at home are often missing from a child's day-care or school experience. This isn't surprising. If you are working with a group of twelve or twenty children, you simply don't have time to listen with interest and offer relevant feedback to what each child is saying. Children respond subtly, and over time, to the experience of getting cut off, asked to hurry, or to find an ending. They respond to the difference between genuine questions that represent the speaker's real desire to find something out and rhetorical ones aimed at eliciting answers the question asker already knows.

Listening attentively to a story is seldom as easy as it sounds, especially with young children. One difference between young children's stories and those of older children and adults is that young children may tell a story with all kinds of interruptions and digressions. Sometimes children begin eager to communicate the story to you. But somewhere in the midst of their narration they become caught up by the telling itself. This may manifest itself through intermittent wordplay within the story, lapses into acting out story sequences with their bodies, use of different voices to convey different characters, or detours into side stories. What began as product oriented—communicating a story—becomes enveloped by the process—the telling itself. Storytelling thus can become a kind of rambling play to the young child. This process can seem boring or aimless to the adult; but from a developmental view, it is vital to the child. The act of telling the story is important for children to develop a love of relating stories and for giving them a full sense of the range of narrative possibilities. Through an immersion in the process of storytelling, children have the opportunity to develop their narrative voice.

Children's Ear for Style

◆

Children obviously do not depend for communication on a knowledge of grammar; they rely on their ear, mostly, which is sharp and quick.

Listening is a two-way street. The construction of children's stories depends as much on what they hear in the stories told them by adults, or ones that they later read, as it does on the feedback they receive. One of the most interesting ways of looking at what children hear in stories is through the lens of genre. The term genre refers to the family of stories—mysteries, romances, or fables—that shares particular subject matter, style, and narrative conventions. Carol Feldman argues that different narrative genres constitute different "epistemic forms," or ways of knowing. To the extent that narrative is a way of understanding human action, one can take different interpretive stances toward it. Different kinds of narratives involve different kinds of insights and knowledge about the protagonist, human actions, and human motivations. Feldman argues that the genre we identify, consciously or unconsciously, guides the way we think about a given story. She suggests that focusing on the feelings and wishes—what she calls the intentional states—of the protagonists, for example, leads to a different reading of a story than does focusing on the intentions of the author.

In a series of studies, Feldman and her students read variations of short stories by Heinrich Böll, Brendan Gill, and the first few pages of Franz Kafka's *The Castle* to undergraduates. In one study, for example, some subjects were read a piece of modern psychologically oriented fiction as it was written, with a focus on consciousness, and some subjects were read the same story, with references to consciousness eliminated. In effect, some people were hearing stories that highlighted the landscape of consciousness, whereas others were hearing stories that highlighted the landscape of action. Feldman and her colleagues then asked questions about the stories, such as what was happening in the story and what might happen to the protagonist in the future.

The subjects seemed very attuned to the genre or landscape they had heard. Those who heard the original versions of the story gave answers that included more terms relating to consciousness, and focused more on the psychological state of the protagonist, than did those who heard the expurgated version. Feldman's work suggests that the way people hear a story being told—the genre they hear—has a formative effect on what they understand of and think about the story, as well as the way they answer questions about it. One way children can develop their own narrative voice is through a kind of borrowing of pieces of what others say in creating their own stories.

Original versus Borrowed Stories

Many children's stories are neither original nor idiosyncratic. Some of the time children ventriloquize—they borrow forms from others and speak the borrowed forms to convey their own experiences. The use of formulas or recognizable styles to express meanings is one powerful way we contribute to communal meanings and shared understanding. Haiku, rap, fables, and newspaper reporting are examples of this. Other forms are somewhat less structured. The short story, for instance, constrained by the valued style of the times, can be rendered using a seemingly infinite array of techniques. Ventriloquizing is as important and useful as creating a new voice or constructing a unique narrative form. For the young child, making use of a well-established form may feel like a new invention or discovery, in the same way that the discovery that a ball continues to exist even when it is hidden feels novel to each infant. We do, however, need to give children plenty of forms and voices to inhabit or borrow. These forms can be introduced in a way that encourages rather than suppresses the development of more individual kinds of story construction.

I videotaped 3, 4, and 5 year olds during their morning circle time at a day-care center. The children were taking turns saying their name and something they wished for. The first child to have a turn spoke up in a husky voice, "My name is Jessie DeRosa, and I wish my mother were dead." A momentary startled silence in the room followed this proclamation. The other children began to take their turns ("I wish it would snow all the time." "I wish I were a bride." "I wish I had a trampoline."). A few kids seemed to like what Jessie had said, and offered variations on that theme ("I wish I were an orphan." "I wish my father were dead." "I wish my brother were dead."). The teachers and I passed over these with little reaction because we assumed that they were manifestations of the kind of copying children delight in, freely borrowing phrases and patterns of response from one another. Soon after that I left.

The next day when I came to videotape again, Lina, the head teacher, came rushing out to talk to me. "You know how Rachel said at circle that she wished her brother was dead? Well, I didn't pay much attention because I thought she was just copying Jessie. But later at nap time I was sitting next to her mat, and she came over and got in my lap and said, 'You know, Lina, when Susan was here and I said that I wished my brother was dead, I really meant it. I do wish he was dead.' And I said, 'Why, Rachel?' And she said, 'Because Daddy always plays with him and never plays with me,' and she went on to tell me about how when she plays with her little baby sister it's always she who gets in trouble. Well, her mother is my sister. And I told her that when I was little and me and Mary used to play I was the one who always got yelled at when there was trouble. And Rachel said, 'And how did that make you feel?' and I said, 'Lousy.'

"Well, I couldn't decide whether to tell her mother, but finally I did tell her what had happened. And there were tears in her eyes, because she felt so awful, and she had had no idea that Rachel was feeling that way. Well, before she could bring it up with Rachel, Rachel told her what had happened. She said to her mom, 'You know today Susan was at school video-taping and she asked us what we wished for and I said I wished Jimmy was dead.' And her mother said, 'Well, I don't think Daddy wants to play dolls with you,' and Rachel told her, 'I don't care if he plays dolls with me, I just want him to play something with me.'"

A powerful set of events was triggered by a simple question, What do you wish for? The questions we ask children are often much more important in their repercussions than we think. A more subtle aspect of this anecdote is that Rachel was inspired by somebody else's phrase. But in borrowing the phrase "I wish my —— was dead," she gave voice to a feeling that was already fermenting inside of her. It's as if I borrowed a friend's dress that was very different from my usual style, and in wearing it some aspects of my personality found expression that otherwise might never have shown themselves.

Linguistically, the idea of ventriloquizing can be related to what Mikhail Bakhtin, John Dore, and James Wertsch all mean by "multivoicedness" or "reinvoicement." Their overlapping ideas all focus on the notion that when we talk, to others or to ourselves (in monologues, in conversations, in writing), we speak through the voices of others. In his analysis of *Crime and Punishment,* for example, Bakhtin demonstrates the ways in which Raskolnikov speaks the "voices" of others and in so doing embodies and represents the experience and consciousness of those around him.

The process of ventriloquization begins in infancy. The child at first internalizes his mother's voice and repeats in his own monologue phrases the mother has used in conversation with him, thus bringing to the child's narratives the ideas, meanings, and forms of the social world around her. As the child develops and becomes more involved with peers and other adults, he also incorporates those voices into his internal monologues and narratives. A narrative is never only the expression of another's consciousness and identity; the speaker speaks through the voices of others. In this way the narrative is always a social construction.

The example of Rachel's ventriloquizing is powerful yet fairly straightforward. She used an expression that appealed to her for two reasons. Children love to mimic each other, borrowing expressions and repeating appealing verbal constructions, and it gave her a form for expressing a feeling she had. By borrowing the phrase, she developed the feeling more fully than she had before, and by saying it to others at circle time she opened the way to saying it to her family, which in turn led to a set of narratives that caused change in the family's dynamic.

If it is true that children develop their own narrative voice in part through the voices they hear and read, what is the nature of that influence? Annie Dillard, in her memoir, *An American Childhood,* recalls this about reading as a child:

> It was clear that adults, including our parents, approved of children who read but it was not at all clear why this

was so. Our reading was subversive, and we knew it. Did they think we read to improve our vocabularies? Did they want us to read and not pay the least bit of heed to what we read, as they wanted us to go to Sunday school and ignore what we heard? . . . What I sought in books was imagination. It was depth, depth of thought and feeling; some sort of extreme of subject matter; some nearness to death; some call to courage. I myself was getting wild; I wanted wildness, originality, genius, rapture, hope. I wanted strength, not tea parties. What I sought in books was a world whose surfaces, whose people and events and days lived, actually matched the exaltation of the interior life. There you could live.

What do children get from the stories they hear or read? What aspects of those stories influence what they themselves write about and how they write? Research and the experience of writers and writing teachers tell us that children's choice of content and the structure of their stories may be explained in a variety of ways. The content of children's stories is usually explained as reconstructions or communications of personal experience, the expression of emotional concerns and interests, and as attempts to make cognitive and affective sense of the world. Psychologists usually explain the structure of children's stories as a manifestation of developmental level and an expression of the internalization of cultural patterns and norms of narrative genre. One aspect of narrative that has received less attention than content or structure is style, or aesthetics, what Dillard means by depth of thought and feeling, originality, and genius.

Researchers typically assess children's internalization of story content and story structure by asking them to repeat or explain a story they have heard. This method presents something of a paradox. On the one hand researchers are examining narrative processes, but they are looking at these processes by eliciting logical, expository, and reflective responses. In these situations children display aspects of their memory and their ability to analyze, interpret, and reorganize the story they have heard. But if we take Bruner's contrast between paradigmatic and narrative ways of thinking seriously, it may be worth trying to understand children's narratives within a narrative mode of inquiry.

Children may best represent their psychological experience of a story with their own story. And they may best reveal what they have taken in or can use from other people's stories by telling their own stories. Characteristics of those stories that mirror or match the stories they heard or read are one indication of what they have internalized. I call this process of repeating and simultaneously subtly transforming what one is repeating *echoing*.

To begin to characterize the different ways in which children echo what they hear, some colleagues and I read stories to more than 100 children between the ages of 5 and 9; then we invited the children to write something of their own—something that the story or poem made them think of or something totally different, anything they liked. The stories and poems we used were all written by well-known adult authors—Emily Dickinson, T. S. Eliot, William Carlos Williams, e e cummings, Sylvia Plath—some of them written for children and others not. The children transformed what they heard in different ways and used the material in their own writing. The type of transformation evident in these writings seemed to fall into three broad groups.

Some of the children turned the material into a traditional narrative. In these cases children used some piece of what they had heard, either the opening sentence or the basic theme or plot, but transformed the structure into a chronologically driven account of their personal experiences. These children replaced the author's content with personal experiences of their own, and replaced the author's tone and plot with their own. For example, in response to "This Is Just to Say" by William Carlos Williams

> *This is Just to say*
> *I have eaten*
> *the plums that were in the icebox*
> *forgive me*
> *they were delicious*
> *so juicy and cold.*

a child wrote:

> *I saw a plum in the icebox. I took the plum out of the icebox. I ate them for breakfast. They tasted very sweet and good. They were good things. I ate four for breakfast. The next morning I got up and ate my breakfast. I had chicken. And I had macaroni and cheese. I had tomato for lunch. Saturday morning I went bowling. That day I went to gymnastics. I saw my mom at the store getting strawberries for our ice cream.*

Very few (only about 5 percent) of the narratives involved this kind of structural transformation. About 10 percent of the children instead imitated much of the structure of what they heard—the form and line configuration as well as the rise and fall of content—but transformed what they had heard either by adding information or emphasizing some detail of feeling. These children, in other words, seemed to borrow what they heard and make it personal. For example, in response to the same Williams poem, another child wrote:

> *I have eaten*
> *the plums*
> *so so sweet and cold*
> *I ate ten of the plums*
> *I was so sorry.*

The vast majority of the children's responses fell into a third category. They were written in a form that suggested that the children were using what they heard as a basis for exploring nontraditional narrative forms. They didn't borrow or imitate the form they heard, but neither did they come up with the stories that are typically produced during writing time at schools. In some of these cases the topic or theme was borrowed, but the use of language and the form of the story or poem were new. For instance:

> *I like plums. They are good. I eat them every day. I squeeze their juice. I crack their bones. I eat every little bit. I love them I say. Well I eat them all day. I love to hear it go squish. They're my favorite kind of food. I hereby declare when I smell the air, I really like it when they go squish. Yes I do.*

Such responses indicate the children's awareness, at some level, that they have heard a departure from conventional storytelling, and they interpret what they have heard as a kind of invitation to depart from their usual forms. Their poems and stories also indicate a striking responsiveness to the aesthetics of what they have heard and a readiness to focus on style in their own work. This was true even of the youngest children in this study. Their response to the material read to them reflects what Carol Feldman would call a genre shift, an ability to move back and forth between different kinds of stories.

The children echoed what they heard in basically five different ways. These types of echoing were not mutually exclusive; some of the pieces included several different types of echoing. Here are some examples.

Content. Some of the children borrowed the content of the story they heard. For instance, in response to "In Only Spring," a story by e e cummings, a child wrote, "In Only Spring I love to jump in mud. It feels so good. I love to take baths and play with my sister. Then we go out."

Theme. In some cases the children responded to the theme rather than the specific content. After hearing *the elephant and the butterfly,* another story by e e cummings, about an elephant and a butterfly who fall in love, a 6-year-old child wrote: "Once there was a boy and his name was Jake. And he was lonely. So he told his friend Tyler and they swung on the hammock." The theme of loneliness and friendship is borrowed, but the child has invented new characters and new events.

Tone. The children were amazingly responsive to the affective tone of the pieces they heard. Often they employed this tone in their own writing even when they used very different forms and language and depicted different kinds of events. For instance, *The Bed Book,* by Sylvia Plath, uses sound and rhythm to convey a lyrical sense of whimsy. Upon hearing it one child wrote: "I wish I was little. I wish I was small, nobody would see me . . . at least not at all. Sick Sick can you pick? Measles, mumps, goose bumps? Do I have a jazzy jazz jazz? Wait listen, quiet, quick! Can you hear the tick tick tick? Hip Hip hooray! it's time to play."

Meter. In a few cases the children borrowed or echoed the meter, which is particularly striking because they didn't see the poems and stories, only listened to them. In some instances, the tone and content were completely different from what they had heard, but the rhythm and configuration of lines seemed to be clearly in response to what they had heard. In response to "In Just Spring" a child wrote: "I thought about sword fighting and daring. As the time comes, people fight and dare. And the swords still come clashing together, as pirate ships move into forts, the war is still on."

Imagery. An aspect of the adult narratives that the children seemed to hear and internalize with particular clarity was the focus on imagery and sensuous detail. For instance in response to "This Is Just to Say," a 7 year old borrowed both the form and the basic idea or vehicle used by Williams. She changed the specific content of the piece but still managed to capture the poet's focus on sensuous experience:

> *I want to say*
> *I have eat the*
> *chicken in the refrigerator.*
> *I hope you don't*
> *mind.*
> *They were so good. The*
> *dark meat and the white*
> *meat.*

In response to "We Like March," by Emily Dickinson, another child changed the topic and the form but kept the focus on imagery: "April is a pool of spring. It's a green world. It's a lake. It's a beautiful world."

In addition, different narratives tended to trigger different kinds of echoing. For instance, the children all heard in Williams's "This Is Just to Say" the unusual phrasing and echoed it even when they departed totally from his theme and content. For example:

> *In the shade of an apple tree*
> *Just you and me*
> *just you and me*

In Dickinson's poem "We Like March," the children heard the unusual phrasing and also captured the essence of the poem, the idea of personalizing the seasons, although they often chose images far different from Dickinson's. For example:

> *He rides the rainbows with a suit of green.*
> *He shades under mushrooms.*
> *He hides around everywhere.*
> *He is very tricky.*
> *He sneaks around the countryside with gold.*
> *He hides in holes.*
> *He is march!*

For the most part, the children's inventions were highly attuned to the characteristics of the specific narrative or poem, and even to the aspect or level of the narrative that was unique or interesting to them. This runs counter to the prevailing idea that children concentrate on content and need to be *trained* to respond to style.

Children respond to the out of the ordinary with out of the ordinary themselves. We often offer children only the conventional and count on their inner processes to restructure and come up with unusual material. Or we count on the individually talented or creative child to shine through. Although many teachers have come to appreciate the value of giving children license to express themselves in journals or open-ended writing activities, they have lost sight of the importance of offering children sources of inspiration.

Children learn their narrative forms from the narratives they hear, are asked about, and encouraged to make. This research suggests that not only is the structure of narrative shaped by cultural forces, but that children respond to style and tone and have an ear for the unusual in language. This is so even for children between the ages of 5 and 10, a stage of development traditionally considered literal, rigid, and rule oriented. The child's grasp of some aspects of the narrative process may form slowly, and over long periods of time, in response to exposure and interaction with external forces (parents, school, literature). But some aspects of the individual child's narrative process are more spontaneous and fluid than is often thought.

Learning about what kinds of narratives children construct requires an appreciation of how sensitive they are to what they hear. This is turn makes it important to take seriously the idea that children are capable of employing a diverse array of narrative styles and techniques to convey what they want to convey. The voice in which we build and tell our story expresses who we are.

7

We Are the Stories We Tell

We trust memory against all evidence: it is selective, subjective, cannily defensive, unreliable as fact. But a single red detail remembered—a hat worn in 1952, the nail polish applied one summer day by an aunt to her toes, separated by balls of cotton, as we watched—has more real blood than the creatures around us on a bus as, for some reason, we think of that day, that hat, those bright feet. That world. This power of memory probably comes from its kinship with the imagination. In memory each of us is an artist: each of us creates. The kingdom of God, the nuns used to tell us in school, is within you. We may not have made religion of memory, but it is our passion, and along with (sometimes in opposition to) science, our authority. It is a kingdom of its own.

If our memory, and the stories we tell about what we remember, make up our kingdom, what determines what kind of kingdom we each inhabit? How do the stories we tell, retell, and listen to contribute to our sense of who we each are?

An 8-year-old boy named Peter insists on having his father tell him the story of his adoption every night before he goes to bed. Peter was born in Korea and was adopted when he was about 8 months old. He arrived in Washington, D.C., by airplane along with many other children who were coming to new families. When the plane landed, all the regular passengers disembarked. Then all the new adoptive parents were brought onto the plane to greet their children. Peter's parents had received a packet of information about him before his arrival, including his photograph. When Peter's father boarded the plane, he was so tall that even though the plane was jammed with officials, flight attendants, and other adults looking for their children, he could see over everyone else's head. He spotted his baby boy immediately, and went right over to him. He recognized his baby. That is the story that Peter wants to hear every night before he sleeps.

We all want to know who we are and how we came into our world. We all want to know that we were recognized, that we are singular and special. And we each learn this, in part, through the stories we are told about our beginnings. No matter what those beginnings may be, no matter what feelings now surround them, they are vital to our sense of who we are. We reencounter ourselves constantly throughout life and confirm what we already know by telling, over and over again, one version or one aspect of the story of our life. Peter's story, in which he was recognized and found by his new father, is a cornerstone of his life story.

If, as Goethe suggested, "Every work is a stepping stone towards a personal confession," the stories children tell are part of the self they are busily constructing. A developmental line runs from the simple autobiographical fragments children describe with their parents when they are 2 to the elaborate fictions they write by themselves when they are, say, 8 years old, and from there on into the future.

So far this book has described some of the functions storytelling serves for the developing child. We have explored the kinds of stories children tell and the paths along which they acquire storytelling abilities. But a central reason it is so important to understand all these whats and hows of storytelling is that the stories play a vital role in shaping children's sense of themselves and their presentation of that self to others.

The preceding chapter demonstrates that the way we tell stories shapes what kind of stories we tell. The same event told two different ways becomes two different stories, with different meanings. The cognitive psychologist Ulric Neisser has argued that an important type of self-knowledge that we construct and refer to daily is what he calls the extended self—the self made up of images or stories of oneself in the past and the future. Through knowledge of our extended self, we can think about enduring and transient aspects of our personality and our experience.

Children are often seen primarily as creatures of action and the moment, rather than as creatures of thought or reflection. We often are drawn to them because of their seeming lack of self-consciousness, "they are who they are" as opposed to adults who can be pretentious, take on airs, remake themselves in an image.

But from an early age children experience themselves though the symbols they use to apprehend, encode, change, and describe experience. This can be done with gesture, with words, and with drawings. But telling stories that capture the flow of experience, in time and space, as a story always does, is perhaps the most essential symbolic process we can use to experience ourselves. It gives us a form in which to create and contemplate the extended self Neisser has described.

Before a child can participate in stories about her experience, she cannot really reflect on herself in the present in relation to herself in the past or the future. It is through the process of narrative construction that she can express and reflect on an identity, a self that has continuity through time and space. While adolescence is the great age for being preoccupied with feelings of "Who am I?" the roots of a sense of self in the world form far earlier in life. These early notions of identity are intimately related to, and flow out of, saying who we are to others and to ourselves through the narratives we construct about our experiences.

Two children can talk about the same event in strikingly different voices. In telling their stories they each contribute to their self-image and at the same time communicate that identity to others. Two 5-year-old cousins have run to the end of the block and back. Upon their return, they tell about the adventure to their mothers. The boy reports: "We ran down to the end of the road. And I got there first. And then we turned around, and we got here in 30 seconds!" The little girl reports: "I said to myself, this is a special day, so don't make a fuss. And so I said to myself, just get on your shoes, and if you get tired don't fuss because you don't want to ruin a special day."

One is telling a story of action, the other is telling a story of thought. One is depicting the outer landscape, the other the inner landscape. The content, what is emphasized, and how it is conveyed shape not only what each child will remember of the experience but also how each child will see him- or herself in that event.

We are who we are by virtue of what we have actually experienced. But part of who we are is determined by what we imagine. Not only because these fantasies express hidden desires, wishes, and fears, but because what we imagine is one facet of our way of thinking, our view of the world, our way of being. In his consideration of the self, William James talks about the possible selves we each construct. Through acts of memory and imagination we depict ourselves as we might be or might have been. We can see ourselves in different roles, doing unusual things, having relationships that don't exist in our current lives. In this sense who we are now is interlaced with the who we might be, the who we would like to be, the who we are afraid of being. Our possible selves contribute to our actual selves, and we construct those possible selves through the stories we tell. Children keep adding to their repertoire of self, then, through the stories they tell about their experience, but also through the stories they tell about what they imagine.

Many psychoanalysts and clinical psychologists have come to view therapy as the process by which we learn to retell the story or stories of our lives. In *Retelling a Life,* Roy Shafer, for example, argues that we construct ourselves through our stories about our own actions, experiences, and relationships. He describes the way in which patients in psychotherapy have the chance, with the help of the therapist, to recast those stories. The therapeutic theories that underlie this new view suggest that the self we try to heal or improve in therapy is the narrated self. The therapist knows only what you tell him about your life, past and present, so that the raw materials of therapy are predominantly stories, not behavior. As you change the way you see yourself, past and present, the stories are transformed. Thus the goal of therapy in this view is not simply to behave differently or to feel differently but to tell a different story about yourself than the one you used to tell. So, for instance, the stories you tell about being a difficult child with whom no one could get along may be retold as stories about a child who was strong willed and looking for someone with whom to connect. The same fragments and core events are reorganized and recast in a way that makes a new story and conveys a new meaning.

Every time you tell a story about yourself, the self depicted becomes available to you as an object of thought or contemplation. It becomes a portrait that you can stand back from and integrate with other stories. You can change it, admire it, recall specific feelings associated with it, and share it with others. Stories are dynamic, modifiable, constructed. Yet each time a story is told it also becomes a text and, therefore, an object that you can reflect on. A piece of information or view of yourself becomes available for you to think about and integrate with other views of yourself. If you tell a story about yourself in which you made someone very happy, you always have that story, that view of yourself, to pull out and look at, and think about. Each time you think about that story or retell it, you become a person who can make people feel happy. In this respect, we are the stories we tell of ourselves.

"As far back as I remember myself (with interest, with amusement, seldom with admiration or disgust . . .)." With this line in *Speak Memory,* Vladimir Nabokov reminds us that we remember ourselves in certain ways more than others, with certain colorations or interpretive stances. Dan McAdams, in his work on the development of a narrative identity, argues that the basis of our interpretive stances, our narrative identity, is set early in life. He draws on the work of Erik Erikson, who suggested that how we resolve fundamental dilemmas of early psychosocial development has an enduring effect on our sense of self. For example, between 18 and 36 months of age, in Erikson's view, issues of dependence and self-control are particularly vivid and turbulent, manifested most dramatically in the struggle over toilet training. Out of that crisis we develop an enduring sense of either autonomy or shame and doubt. McAdams argues that the way in which a child resolves this crisis pervades later narratives of the self. For example, a child who develops a strong sense of inadequacy and shame during this phase is likely to tell stories about himself when he is older that convey in tone, if not in substance, a sense of shame and inadequacy about the self.

Nabokov tells of a vivid memory involving his mother, his brother, and himself at Christmas time:

> One Christmas eve, in Vyra, not long before her fourth baby was to be born, she happened to be laid up with a slight ailment and made my brother and me (aged, respectively, five and six) promise not to look into the Christmas stockings that we would find hanging from our bedposts on the following morning but to bring them over to her room and investigate them there, so that she could watch and enjoy our pleasure. Upon awakening, I held a furtive conference with my brother, after which, with eager hands, each felt his delightfully crackling stocking, stuffed with small presents; these we cautiously fished out one by one, undid the ribbons, loosened the tissue paper, inspected everything by the weak light that came through a chink in the shutters, wrapped up the little things again, and crammed them back where they had been. I next recall our sitting on our mother's bed, holding those lumpy stockings and doing our best to give the performance she had wanted to see; but we had so messed up the wrappings, so amateurish were our renderings of enthusiastic surprise (I can see my brother casting his eyes upward and exclaiming, in imitation of our new french governess, "Ah, que c'est beau!"), that, after observing us for a moment, our audience burst into tears. A decade passed. World War One started.

Nabokov made his mother cry, and her tears mortified him. The story shapes his conception of himself within his family. And his mother's disappointment still looms large: Compare the space given to describing that sequence to the passing of the subsequent ten years in one sentence.

The way that stories shape who we are changes over the course of development. It seems to pass through five developmental phases, each phase incorporating the character-istics of the phase before it. In each phase, children are engaged in a dynamic process in which they use stories to create, experi-ence, and communicate who they are. But the thrust of this enterprise shifts as they acquire new abilities. Describing the changing relationship between self and story as a series of phases is not meant to imply that we leap from one phase to another or that these phases are ironclad in their elements or mutually exclusive. But seeing narrative development in a sequence of such phases can help us to see how dynamic the vital relationship between story and self is. As babies become children, and children, adults, their skills change and build on one another. Their interests and concerns shift and incorporate old interests and concerns, and their way of relating to the outside world changes. Children use stories to widen their social world, and in turn their use and style of telling stories reflects their expanding relationships within the social world. These developmental transitions affect how we construct ourselves in stories and how we communicate a sense of self to others through stories.

Phase 1:
The Emergence of Self in Stories

◆

Right from the start mothers tell children stories about them-selves and invite their children to participate in these stories. A mother and her 18-month-old child are looking at a photo album together, and the mother says: "You were there. You were 3 months old. Remember that? Remember that? That was the first weekend you spent the night like a good girl."

This mother's expectation of her daughter's recall has some of the seeming absurdity of Halliday's contention that his 2-month-old son Nigel wanted to tell him about the miserable inoculation he had been subjected to. But her commentary contains an important lesson for us, and an important lesson for the child. The lesson for us is that parents direct their child's attention to the extended self before this has become an active form of accumulating self-knowledge for the child on his or her own. Parents, as shown in Chapter 5, construct forms of expression and experience in anticipation of their children becoming ready to master these processes independently. The lesson for the child is more personal and far reaching. The mother is saying to her child: You are a part of things that have happened. We can talk about those experiences, and we can gain insight about who you were and who you are through the stories we tell. The mother says it explicitly: This picture is from something that happened and "you were there." You are capable of having a memory and thinking about it. "Remember that? Remember that?" You did something at that time worth recalling and talking about, something that affected all of us. "That was the first weekend you slept the whole night." By reflecting on your actions we can evaluate you, past and present, "like a good girl."

The first stage, then, in using stories to construct a self is a participatory one, where children are as often as not the audience to their parent's stories about them. At this initial stage, what toddlers are learning is that they have a past, that it can be described, and that it is a way for themselves and others to know and to think about who they are. With their parents they are learning that they have an extended self, one that can take on all kinds of affective tones and meanings.

Phase 2:
Creating the Past with Parents

By the time children are 3 they have become masterful talkers, with a burgeoning sense of the power of language not only to name and request things but also to entertain, anger, and delight those around them. They can now use language to express feelings and thoughts. At the same time they are engaged in a dramatic exploration of their uniqueness. This exploration builds on their surer sense of themselves as having a cohesive and interesting extended self. They are less dependent on their parents to construct basic references to the past; they can now do this more on their own. Parents, however, have become vital partners in describing past experiences to fill out their children's sense of themselves over time.

A father and his 3 year old are looking at pictures in a magazine. "This reminds me of a building we made a few months ago," the father says. "Remember that big building we made with blocks?" The 3 year old looks up with rapt attention. The father continues, "Remember? We had towers like that too. And you wanted to make it higher and higher. Remember that? And I kept saying, 'I don't know, Jason. It might fall down.'"

Jason looks at his father, and his expression flickers. "Yeah. It fell. And I cried." His father responds, "Yeah, you were sad because it fell. But I said, 'Don't worry, we can build it back.' And so we started building again, only this time we made the towers wider so they wouldn't fall down. And you were so happy because it was so big and huge. And we made the towers higher and it didn't fall down. It was beautiful and everyone told us it was beautiful. We left it up for days. Remember? And I think it looked like the one in this picture."

This story is as much about connections as it is about the triumph of the tall buildings. The father is linking what he and his son are doing now, looking at pictures, with what they did months ago. He is strengthening the little boy's album of "things I do with my father," and at the same time the boy and his father are reliving an experience important to them. It is a story about them as a team, told by them as a team in the context of being together again. This child is learning what goes into an evocative description of past experience; at the same time he is reexperiencing himself in a way that highlights certain characteristics of his life.

By the time children are 3 they are quite capable of telling stories with others and even on their own. While they are still affirming that they existed in the past and that that past self is related to their current self, they are also branching out, focusing more (with their parents) on the themes, emotional tones, and details of the stories. They are beginning to explore, probably without realizing it, the self-constructive potential of personal stories.

The stories children hear told about themselves to others, by their parents, also contribute to their sense of self. Usually if your children are nearby when you tell a favorite story about them to another adult, they will look on as a secondary audience. Although they experienced whatever is being described, and no doubt have heard the tale about the experience already, maybe several times before, they listen again, often attentively, sometimes ruefully. They are taking in your version of who they are. And there is a good chance that someday they will recount the story themselves, capturing your tone, your perspective, perhaps with a commentary on your telling.

Stories not only help shape how a person sees himself, they also may influence how others see that person, which can further affect how he sees himself. Neal, an acquaintance's 4-year-old son, fell and got a deep cut near his lip. His parents took him to the doctor, who said that he would need a tetanus shot and then they would have to go to a nearby hospital for a plastic surgeon to put stitches in. Neal appeared very calm and almost unaware of what the doctor had said. So much so that after the shot, which he didn't like, he seemed relieved and elated. He was so happy scrambling into the car that his mother, concerned that he didn't realize he had more of the ordeal ahead of him, said, "Neal, we have one more thing we have to do. We have to go see another doctor who will put stitches in. And then we will be through." He said quietly, "I know." The stitching was quite traumatic, but he was very brave.

Later his mother talked about it to the family and friends, so Neal heard her repeat the story several times. About the third time he said, when she finished, "You know, Mom, when the doctor told you I was going to need to go to the emergency room to have stitches I almost cried. But I didn't." He had understood, and what she had taken for blithe nonawareness had actually been a supreme effort at bravery. He heard her story of the incident and added something to it that changed the meaning of the story and of the event for both of them. His insight about the experience then became part of the story his mother told to her friends. Together Neal and his mother had constructed a story that revealed how they both experienced the event. He also now has a story for his repertoire of self, in which he bravely suffers a traumatic event and covers up his feelings. And in hearing his mother retell it to others he gets some sense of its significance, some sense of what it showed his mother about him.

The social contexts in which children tell stories not only facilitate talk about the personal past, but social interactions are the process by which the personal past is formulated into narratives. Peggy Miller collected personal narratives that children between the ages of 2 and 5 told conjointly with siblings, parents, or other family members. Miller argues that in joint storytelling there are two levels on which children represent themselves interpersonally. The first is the relationship to others described in the story: "At the picnic, Jordan and I were wrestling, and he knocked me to the ground, but I know more wrestling than he does, so I flipped him over." The second is the relationship to others created through the telling: "Remember when we were in kindergarten?" "Yeah, and we used to play that game puppy dog?"

Children also use stories of their past to portray their feelings about events. Miller was surprised at the high degree of interpretation of emotion that the children she studied included in their narratives. Interestingly, she found that the huge predominance of stories about the specific past that young children told their caregivers was about negative experiences (getting hurt, being frightened, and the like). She suggests that this may be because they have heard adults talking about negative experiences, and that they have learned this is one way to gain the floor. In addition, by talking about negative experiences they can get comfort and reassurance. For instance, one little girl tells about falling, but not about the kiss she got for falling, and instead gets a kiss while telling the story.

Our stories always have a communicative aspect, always an intended audience, even if we are our own audience (and we always are, even if there is another audience). All symbols, including the words we use to create stories, are inherently communicative. They must be heard, read, or understood by another. In telling about ourselves, we thus not only create ourselves but are simultaneously created by the others who hear our stories. When children tell stories about their past to and with their parents, not only do the parents' specific contributions help shape the content of those stories, but their role as audience affects what children put into the story. The child may include details that will please a parent, attract his attention, or provoke him. The child's sense of his listener will end up influencing what goes into the story and how it gets told. Ultimately, that story will contribute to the child's inner sense of self.

Phase 3:
The Self Shared with Young Friends

◆

While early on a lot of talk about the self occurs within the familiar and highly structured context of parent-child conversation, as children get to be 3, 4, and 5 years of age, they increasingly branch out, forming relationships with friends and other adults. Their sense of story becomes more firmly internalized, allowing them to begin to tell stories in a wider variety of situations besides those with their parents. At the same time they spend increasingly more of their time with peers, whether in informal settings or day-care centers. Whereas an infant's and toddler's emerging identity grows mainly out of the parent-child bond and the parents' behavior toward their child, a 3 or 4 year old begins to discover more and more about herself in relation to other children. The expanding circle in which children use stories is manifested in the number and variety of stories and narrative fragments that can be identified in group settings for preschool children. In fifteen minutes of recording at one day-care center, for instance, we recorded these stories or fragments of stories:

One little girl said to another: "Hey, you know what my mom and dad used to call me?" *(then they disappeared under the table where the tale continued)*

A girl told her teacher about a time when her parents went on a trip and she stayed home with her big sister.

Two boys playing in the sand began to construct a history of their characters, "Let's pretend that once a very old man lived here."

A girl reported that her parents had just bought her a new little kitten.

A preschooler's identity begins to draw on feedback she gets from those she plays with. Preschoolers are highly motivated to coordinate their play with others. They are building true friendships and developing favorite activities with specific other children. Fights, allegiances, competition, successful collaboration, and the responses of other children take on an increasingly important role in how a child sees herself.

One primary way that children communicate with one another within play settings is through the stories they tell to and with each other. Children of this age use stories to share themselves with their friends. The fact that they are now at a stage where they are likely to interweave fact and fantasy offers them opportunities for presenting themselves as they would like to be seen by their peers. A 4 year old turns to the group during morning meeting time at nursery school and tells his friends and teacher: "Last night a mouse fell right onto my mom's lap. It fell right out of the ceiling. My mom was so scared she jumped up onto a chair. And she screamed. Loud." The teacher says, "Were you scared?" The boy responds, "No way! I'm not scared of mice. And I'm not scared of bats. I love bats. I wanted to catch one and keep it for a pet."

Children of 3 and 4 also present themselves to one another through the identities they create in their pretend play narratives. For instance, in a family day-care setting one 4 year old consistently enacts a benevolent and beautiful fairy princess. But she keeps modifying this role so that it can be coordinated with her friend's favorite role, that of a baby horse. The language they use to narrate this evolving game constitutes an ongoing story featuring the collective adventures of the princess and the horse.

Whereas play is the main stuff of 3 and 4 year old's peer relationships, by age 5 good friends spend a great deal of their time together talking about what they will play—often leaving little time for carrying out their plans. By 6 or 7 many children spend most of their time talking about what they like and don't like—about similarities and differences between their classes—and trading stories. They especially seem to relish shared experiences:

"*Remember when we made that hideout?*"
"*Yeah. And you got knocked in the head with the branch?*"
"*Yeah* (delighted laughter), *and I didn't feel anything and you looked at me—and you were screaming . . .*"
"*Yeah. And Davey went running for my mother.*"

By recounting together a shared experience these children are strengthening their intimacy. Every time you tell a story with people close to you about a shared experience, and they agree emphatically with your telling, they are confirming your relationship and your experience of the event, and thus confirming you. Which is perhaps why when another family member challenges your version of an event, you feel anger. When your story is disconfirmed, it seems that you are being disconfirmed. Young children get very upset if they ask if you remember something that happened and you say that you don't remember it. I used to think that this was because they felt that their cognitive abilities, their hold on reality, was being challenged. This is probably true. But I've come to believe that it is also because you are challenging their personal history.

And that is treading on dynamite—even among adults. Listen to members of a family, all grown, discuss whether some particular event happened the way the mother remembers it or the way the sister or brother remembers it. Disagreements over the sequence and details of past events evoke a great deal of feeling. Why? Not only because the disagreement may be about something that symbolizes areas of discord or long-brewing tensions within the family, but because each person feels that his sense of self, his sense of personal past is being challenged.

While we are more accustomed to the notion that children develop their identity in part through and with their parents, it can be less apparent that young children develop and confirm their identity through and with their friends. But the prevalence and variety of stories children tell with one another, and the excitement with which they do it, attest to the importance of shared narratives as a source of identity formation.

Phase 4:
The Self Constructed Through Many Stories
◆

By the time children are 5 or 6 they have accumulated a repertoire of stories of the self, have developed some favorite stories, and may work on an extended oral or written story. They may return over and over again to the same story in their play, and they may build on it from one play session to another. Favorite plots, characters, or themes may be incorporated over and over into a series of stories a 6 year old might tell. By this age children are likely to have been exposed to a variety of story types or genres. They may choose one that best suits the story or stories they feel compelled to tell and keep reusing that genre to express some underlying set of related ideas or feelings. Because children in this age group are so much less rooted in the here and now, they carry around with them a cohesive, if shifting, sense of an inner self and an extended self.

Because of these developmental shifts, children beyond the age of 5 are more likely to tell stories that may have different forms and content but which contain underlying connections and themes that reinforce and contribute to their sense of self. They have an increased capacity to hold different ideas in their mind at the same time and to return again and again to a topic or theme to continue thinking about it or telling a story about it. In this way, their stories begin to form a body of work that creates and depicts the self in a deeper, more multifaceted manner than any one story might be capable of conveying.

Whereas 2 year olds use stories to understand the social world contained in their immediate family life, children 7, 8, and 9 years old use collections of stories and ongoing sagas to penetrate the complexities of the expanded, more complex social world in which they are now active. This is vividly demonstrated in Carolyn Steedman's analysis of a story written by three 8-year-old British girls over the course of several days. The story, and the girls' recorded discussions while writing the story, revolve around the domestic concerns and adventures of several fictional families. Social class, money, and child rearing are recurrent themes in the story. The girls needed the time and the group discussions in order to use the process of writing the story as a means of understanding their society, and thus themselves.

As children grow older and become active participants in the complexities of the larger social world, their repertoire of favorite stories and story types becomes correspondingly larger and more multifaceted. They become better able to tell a variety of different kinds of stories. Most adults will tell different stories in different situations. The story you tell at a party to make people laugh might be mildly self-deprecating, whereas the story you tell at an interview or on a date might be mildly self-aggrandizing. Children are as capable of this situational flexibility as an adult, especially by the age of 8 or 9. And yet, as any therapist will tell you, there is some cohesion to a person's repertoire that offers hints about how that person sees himself and how he wants to present himself. As William James pointed out in his explorations of the self, we are at once a stable self with some sense of an inner identity that has coherence and identity, and at the same time we are many selves, varying across situation and time. Children's inner core identity emerges and strengthens, and at the same time they begin to branch out into the world and try out the many selves required of social beings. Their stories realize this dual aspect of the self.

Consider, for example, two stories written by an 8-year-old boy within a one-month period. The first story was written in response to an assignment on the first day of school and is titled "My Travels." It highlights what was important to him about his summer experience and also captures the self he wants others in his new class to know about. Both in content and tone it shapes a school identity. In contrast, the second story was written at home with an admired grown-up friend, a filmmaker, and is titled "The Monster That Tries to Eat Hollywood: Volcano Man." It is much more rambling and also more dramatic. It is part of this child's imagined self, the one he would like his admired friend to know about, the self elicited by this friend.

Not only are the themes of the two stories different, but the voice the young narrator employs differs in his two stories as well. The story of his summer is told in simple, clear language, specifying important information about where and what he did, "We wanted to go tubing very badly, but we never got a chance to. Instead, we went to the river where we were going to go tubing on, and we caught minnows with a minnow net. . . . Then we went home to have a big long rest." In contrast, consider the following lines from his work of fiction: "Once there was a volcano in LA. It blew up. A scientist made this giant barrel of green slime and the lava blew it up. When the slime and lava met they made a giant volcano man. It grew to be one hundred and fifteen feet and started eating cars, guzzling down people. It was a terror. People were running and screaming. Children were climbing on it and getting burned to toast . . . the director said 'PUT THIS ON MOVIE.'" There is a logic and prosaic quality to the self he communicates, appropriate for sharing with a teacher and new schoolmates. His work of fiction however, is less organized, more playfully told, and reveals his more chaotic, explosive self.

As just suggested, by the time children are school-aged, the self manifests itself in a wide variety of stories, from informal conversational fragments between two children or adult and child, to the more formal stories written in school. The self may come through the content, and/or the style, or narrative voice. Children may use different genres to express different aspects of the self. Storytelling may in itself constitute a statement of personal identity: I am a person who tells lots of stories that other children love to hear. At this stage there is much more potential for the suppression or facilitation of expressing the self through stories, depending on the environment in which the child tells stories and the feedback she or he receives.

Phase 5:
Crystallization of the Childhood Self

The act of storytelling seems to dwindle during the school years. An observer at a playground of first to sixth graders will hear fewer and fewer children making up stories with one another as a form of play. Telling and writing stories diminishes as a vital part of daily school activities. A 9 year old spends less time than she used to eagerly entertaining her parents with reminiscences from the recent or distant past. We simply are less avid storytellers as we grow up. But we do begin to refine and rehearse a collection of stories about ourselves that continues to define us for ourselves and for our friends and acquaintances.

Adults usually remember a few stories from their childhood that encapsulate the way they view their childhood and often reveal how they feel they were viewed by their parents. These stories are usually a blend of actual memories, rehearsed and retold, and versions of the story told to them by their own parents. It is a shared myth of childhood; but as with most myths, it may contain important or emotional points of the truth. A man tells a story of his toddlerhood that he assumes was told to him repeatedly since he remembers almost nothing else of that period. The story/memory is that when he was little he only learned to walk using a cane belonging to some relatives. He wouldn't try walking without it, depending upon it to go everywhere. But, so the story goes, his parents "really fooled him." They exchanged the cane for a clothes pin. And he accepted the substitution, walking around the house holding the clothespin. Obviously the pin didn't give him any support, so they had weaned him from his dependence on the cane without his knowing it. But it is also clear in his retelling of this story that they felt a kind of scornful amusement at him for being duped and that he feels humiliated at having been duped and perceived as being duped, in that way. Probably all of us have family stories like that about our childhood that reveal how we view our childhood and how we think our family viewed us as children.

Clearly, many of the things I have said about how children construct and express who they are through their stories holds true for adults. Their sense of self in stories is not confined to stories of their childhood. But the developmental trajectory I have just described suggests that in addition to the myriad ways in which the adult conveys himself through his stories, the stories recalled from childhood, perhaps first told in childhood, have their own importance in terms of the overall sense of self and life story that the individual constructs and draws upon in everyday experience.

Adults recalling their childhood say that they observe their past self much as they observe a child on a playground, as somehow both separate and living from a wholly different perspective. The self in their stories, like the child on the playground, inhabits a somewhat foreign land. Adults vary with respect to how much they remember of the child they were. The stories they tell about their childhood reflect this; some are told in the voice of the child, others clearly from an adult perspective. Some are told with a graphic immediacy, and others convey a sense of great distance, a kind of muting of the long-ago past. Narrative qualities such as these both reflect and contribute to the adult's sense of connection with his childhood.

8

♦

Fostering Narrative Development

♦

In this book I have tried to identify the developmental sources of children's narrative activity. Some aspects of narrative involve unfolding abilities that seem more or less universal in their prevalence and the ease and invariability with which they emerge. For instance, almost all children verbally sequence their experience. By the time they are 3 years old, they can talk about what happens first, what comes next, and what happens after that, a prerequisite for narrative construction. And they seem almost inevitably to describe experience in terms of where it happened (place) and when it happened (time), two other prerequisites of narrative construction. By the age of 5, virtually all children can refer to the past and the future in the proper tenses. Almost all children come to be able to include an opening, a high point, and an ending to their stories when asked to do so; some children do it even when they are not required to.

Other aspects of storytelling vary with the cultural values and habits of the child's community. Even these characteristics, though, like the more formal ones mentioned above, seem accessible to most children within a community. For instance, a child who grows up in a community that stresses the moral message inherent in a good story is likely to be able to pinpoint the message in someone else's story and be able to produce a story of a similar type. If, on the other hand, a community values the sharing of the inner self through stories, children in that community are more likely to include first-person material in their own stories, more likely to comment, explicitly or implicitly, on the personal meaning of a story, and to respond to first-person material in the stories of other children. In all communities children learn to tell stories in order to become full participants in their community and to develop relationships with other people, as much as they do to formulate experience for themselves.

Still other characteristics of storytelling seem more fragile, more dependent on the individual child's specific environment. A child's sense of freedom to use language in new ways to express his or her particular meaning is something that can flourish or dim, depending on the environment. The development of a narrative voice that communicates unique experience and perspective is more apparent in some children than in others. A child's sense that he can reflect on his past and use this capacity to gain insights about himself can be eclipsed or encouraged and expanded.

One of the things I have tried to show is that stories are not merely a nice or fun decoration added to the real stuff of mental development. They *are,* in many respects, the real stuff of mental development. The construction, telling, and retelling of stories allow children to learn about their world and reflect on their knowledge. The making of stories also allows them to know themselves; through stories, children construct a self and communicate that self to others.

Given the importance of storytelling in early life, what enables children to develop a strong sense of personal narrative? I think two characteristics are fundamental—confidence and joyousness in telling stories. Children should feel that their stories successfully communicate their specific meaning, whether it is real experience or fantasy. Ideally, a child should be able to talk about his experiences and fantasies in a distinctive style, aesthetic, and structure that convey his particular memories, ideas, and feelings. If a child feels both joyous and confident, he or she is much more likely to exploit storytelling and story writing as a means of constructing and communicating experience and ideas. The richer his repertoire of narrative genres and storytelling vocabulary, the more competent and powerful he will be both in reflecting on experience and in sharing experience and communicating with others. No small accomplishments in a world where we despair at the decline of literacy and the decline of discussion as a means of learning and solving problems.

To develop and maintain joy and confidence involves a kind of narrative literacy and love of the process of narrative. I believe that this comes naturally to children because I think it is an essential aspect of what it means to be a human being. The irony is that through instruction, informal and formal, we tend to weed it out. No one consciously tries to squelch his child's or his student's storytelling. Often we correct, refocus, and query because we want to teach our children a better way to do it; we want to help them develop their narrative ability. Just as it seems natural to correct a child's grammar when it is incorrect, the ways in which we respond to children's stories are often meant to help. We may be unaware of how we hinder the process.

I am not suggesting that children naturally have all they need and that instruction is simply a process of ruining a good thing. This is not a modern-day Rousseau argument. There is a difference between thinking that children are budding fine artists and thinking that there is a developmental continuity between what young children do and what adults, especially great writers, are capable of. It is a pretentious cliché to say that children are great artists, naturally creative, and that they just need free rein to realize this potential for greatness. On the other hand, we tend to underestimate what children's stories contain, and we often neglect the emerging aesthetic and personal voice in their stories.

The neglect comes from two different sources. The first is an overemphasis on the "correctness" of children's stories, the purely cognitive aspects (if there is any such thing) that are developed and expressed through narratives. So adults, whether they be parents, teachers, or researchers, may attend to such phenomena as proper grammar, the ability to control tense or to express logical relatedness, at the expense of the emerging meaning or aesthetic that may at times cloud or be clouded by such cognitive demands. For instance, a child's impulse to convey the actual and/or logical sequence of events may conflict with his desire to organize events in terms of their personal significance and meaning. The adult, in an effort to identify aspects of cognitive development, may treat aesthetic maneuvers as noise, to be filtered out, or looked through. A teacher of a 5 year old, interested in helping her learn to sequence or learn the difference between fact and fiction, may discourage characteristics of the story that are actually integral parts of its fabric and tone.

The second source of aesthetic and imaginative neglect derives from the common assumption that the young child's inventions are merely childish. They are often viewed as simply cute, as an amusing artifact of the child's immaturity, rather than as a crucial step toward a fundamental ability in adult life. When *that* is the source of neglect, teachers and parents may even encourage the young child's quirky, fanciful, or odd story but are unlikely to hear it as the expression of an emerging voice intent on conveying personal meaning and complexity.

Not all young children are budding Charles Dickenses. But at least, theoretically, there is a relationship between every child's informal spur-of-the-moment constructions and the carefully crafted work of the novelist. We love great novels because they are the zenith of what we all do in partial ways throughout our lives. The gap wouldn't be as great as it often is if we attended more to the strands that form a bridge between the young child and the great novelist.

What can we as parents, teachers, and other adults do to encourage the development of both a love for and an ability to tell stories? Here are six suggestions.

Listen Attentively

Children are rarely listened to as if what they had to say was meaningful, informative, and interesting. The listener has an important effect, not just on the feelings of the teller but on the story itself. All narratives are constructed in terms of some real or imagined listener. An active, present listener who responds substantively can have two levels of effect on the teller's story. First, when children know that someone is listening with interest, they feel pleased, motivated to continue, encouraged to express themselves. Any parent or teacher is familiar with the fervent request: "Watch this. Watch me!" Many parents and teachers have laughingly commented that children need to be watched in order to grow. If this is true of watching, it is certainly true of listening. Listening helps children develop even when you don't say anything.

Second, at a more concrete level, smiles, contemplative looks, gasps, murmurs, and repetitions can cause the teller to elaborate, shorten, redirect, tighten the tempo, add outrageous language. The listener helps shape the story. Assume that you have something interesting and important to find out from your child's story, whether it's information about her day, insight into how she feels about the world, a sense of how she organizes her experience, or how she puts a story together. Assume she is an interesting, complex, and worthwhile conversational partner, and that her story holds as many riches as that of any other member of the community. Listening in this way will make it a great deal more likely that she will tell interesting, complex, and worthwhile stories. It will turn the storytelling situation into a setting for rich development.

Respond Substantively

◆

Part of listening well is responding appropriately. If a child has something valuable to say, it's reasonable that we will have meaningful reactions and responses. Interestingly, teachers tend to respond in terms of explicit scaffolding, or teaching questions. For instance, a 3 year old says to his teacher, "I went to the fair this weekend, and it was lots of sheep there," and his teacher responds, "There were lots of sheep there?" The emphasis of this teacher's response is on correcting her student's grammar. Moreover, she does not show the storyteller that she is truly interested in learning more about the child's experience at the fair.

If you listen to a child's story with an ear to correcting it or improving it, you will offer one set of responses, not necessarily the most enriching or engaging. If, on the other hand, you listen in the same way that you would to any story you were eager to hear, then you are much more likely to ask questions that reflect genuine, specific attention and interest. You also might respond with a story of your own, which is a powerful way of sharing a storytelling activity.

Teachers' concerns with making activities "educational" sometimes prevent them from responding in a way that would be even more genuinely educational. That is, in their efforts to teach specific skills such as sequencing and good grammar, and their attention to correcting children's mistakes, they often fail to respond to the more meaningful aspects of the story. In so doing they often miss the opportunity to respond in a more spontaneous and substantive manner, which would expand and enrich the aspect of the activity that really matters, the child's ability to express personal meaning with his stories.

Rich, complex, engaged conversations are apt to provide as much or more educational material for a young child as more pedagogically structured interactions. As children get older, and write more of their stories, the same kind of response is possible in a different form. One can respond to the story more as a member of an interested audience than as an evaluator. When one responds as a member of an audience, one is likely to ask for more detail (What kind of dress was she wearing? How old was he when he ran away?) or for clarification (Did all of the monsters die?). In taking the role of listener seriously, one gives a different kind of feedback than by merely listening for what can be improved according to some static or set criteria.

Collaborate

◆

Many of us collaborate when we are telling stories with toddlers without realizing it. Without the collaboration they wouldn't tell many stories. But as children get older we tend to think we should stay out of their stories, let them do it themselves. Research shows that, whether we mean to or not, our response shapes their narrative. So why not really collaborate, rather than assume that you are on such a different level you can't tell stories together. These collaborations can take several forms, just as they do earlier in a child's life. The adult can ask questions that shape and direct what the child puts into her story, he can add a piece to the story, or he can include his child's contributions in his story.

A mother is sitting with her daughter and her niece, both of whom are 5. The mother had recently told her daughter a story in which the niece and her mother had heard a strange noise in the middle of the night and discovered that it was a talking troll doll whose battery had gone haywire. When the little girl, her cousin, and her mother sat down together, the daughter turned to her mother and said, "Tell me the story about the troll again." So the mother began, "Well the other night Simone and her mother were asleep. Then suddenly they heard a strange noise in the night." At this point, Simone breaks in, "And we heard it in our minds!" So the mother continues, "They heard a strange noise in the middle of the night, and in their minds." The collaboration improves the story for all.

On a class visit to a museum, a group of second graders was asked to make up a story about a painting. The group leader, uncertain how to begin (although she herself had told them several good stories about other paintings), said, "Well, let's see. What do you think is going on here?" There was a long silence, and then one of the children said, "The horses are drinking water." The teacher, not satisfied that this was the beginning of a story, said, "OK. Well, where do you think these people are from?" and the kids shouted, "Paris!!!" "Egypt!!!" "India!!" The teacher looked crestfallen that this also had not begun the story. A second teacher stepped in and said, "Let's make up a story. How shall our story begin?" The children responded:

> Many years ago there was a city in a faraway land. And people lived there. There were palm trees and it was very hot and they needed lots of water. But the water kept drying up. They were getting hungry and thirsty. They didn't have much for the babies. This guy came over and he said, "We have to block the sun. We should get a big thing to cover the sun—and whoever can find something big enough will win a prize." They looked everywhere. One man named George went to France and found a huge sheet. But he couldn't find anything to hang it. But he found a balloon, and he blew it up, he found some string, he tied it on—the sun started to go away. And it started to snow.

Different questions lead to different stories, as do different situations. In this case the teacher serves as collaborator by offering a jumping-off point, one that is within a story framework, "How shall we begin?" In effect, she has invited the children to take a narrative stance toward the subject matter. The group leader's questions, while perfectly reasonable, are outside of the story framework and therefore do not prompt a story response. By entering into the fray, as it were, the second teacher becomes part of a narrative effort that yields a good story for all.

Provide a Multiplicity of Voices and Genres

When it comes to assimilating different styles of storytelling, research has shown that children have amazingly open and responsive ears. They may even be more attuned to this than older people. As young language learners, they are extremely sensitive to unusual verbal constructions in order to learn what is appropriate and what their options are. This may be why children so readily learn the forms for rap, riddles, or knock-knock jokes. In fact, children often learn a genre, format, or narrative technique before they learn the appropriate content (listen to a kid's first knock-knock jokes, for instance). In other words, they frequently hear the tune before they hear the words, but they are ready and eager to employ what poets have called "a generosity of language."

If children are surrounded with a multiplicity of styles, they are likely to have a wide repertoire from which to choose for their own stories. It is important for teachers and parents to choose stories and poems to read to kids because they have beautiful language in them or are told in an unusual way, not simply because the content of the story is appropriate. You need not be constrained by what you think your children or students will understand. As first language learners, they heard an enormous amount of language that they didn't understand.

In some respects that's how they got into the language initially. Children take in much more than they can immediately comprehend, or comprehend in an adult way. Even if a work is beyond them, that doesn't mean that they won't find it interesting, meaningful, or important in the moment, or that they won't make use of it later on.

We tend to reserve great stories and poems until we think children are old enough to appreciate them. Instead, assume that if they start hearing beautiful language, well-constructed narratives, and different genres early in life, they will acquire a vocabulary of narrative in the same way that they seem so easily to acquire a vocabulary of words. They don't need to tell you what it was about or to correctly answer your questions in order to have learned something from it. Sometimes the effect shows up much later in what they produce, rather than in their answers to your immediate queries. If the meaning is complex or subtle, but the children like it, read it again and again. Children, like adults, often want to hear something several times, especially if they think it is beautiful, disturbing, or interesting, even though hard to grasp fully.

Encourage the Use of a Wide Range of Story Forms

◆

I overheard a kindergarten teacher telling a parent that her goal for the year was to teach the children how to make stories with a beginning, middle, and end. This impulse is similar to feeling that you have to teach children that sentences have structure. Children often don't need to be taught this; they extract it from what they hear and use that structure to organize their thoughts. They do it on their own, if they are exposed to stories and have any semblance of ordered events within their own lives. They need two things in school: plenty of chances to tell stories and lots of freedom to tell stories the way they want to. Before correcting a child's story, before requesting that it be made longer, clearer, more accurate, or more logical, read it for what it tells you, as it is written (or told). Assume it says what the child wants to say. Then suggest corrections, if necessary.

There are two equally important reasons for teachers to value a diverse array of narrative styles and voices. One is that it encourages children to build more textured and deeply felt ways of telling what they want to say and builds a richer repertoire of styles, thus developing narrative literacy. The second reason is that the students probably come from diverse home lives and communities. They may be learning very different narrative values at home. By overlooking these in teaching mainstream school narrative values, you may squelch their narrative impulse altogether. The child who is not encouraged to use his family's narrative style at school may, as a result, have trouble learning the school narrative style. Like a person who immigrates to a new country, he may abandon his native language while never fully learning the language of his adopted country, and thus become a person without a language of his own. If storytelling is as central to thinking and communicating as it appears to be, imagine the effect on the child who has no strong vibrant narrative style.

Even if the children come from a homogeneous background and have no trouble learning the school narrative style, there is every reason to encourage a wide array of genres and styles. By school style, I mean a style that emphasizes the preeminence of a conventional structure and grammatical correctness at the expense of evocativeness and, in many cases, emotional veracity. Often the school style has little aesthetic merit and is completely inadequate for expressing personal, unusual, or powerful experience. It is often lacking in the deep aesthetic range that is necessary to communicate meaningful events and ideas. Children need to find their own voice, even if that voice is constructed as a patchwork of styles and themes running through things they have heard.

This suggestion is not to be confused with the idea prevalent in many preschools and elementary grades that anything a child writes is wonderful. Open-ended is not the same as aesthetically enriched. For more than a decade more and more teachers have embraced the practice of giving their students opportunities to draw and write freely, without a prescribed formula.

For example, based on the Writing Workshop ideas described by Donald Graves, many teachers have their children write about anything they want in a daily journal or folder. The children then use these spontaneous and varied writing samples as the basis for more deliberate, crafted pieces of writing. As a process for getting children to feel comfortable writing and as a way of letting kids know there are lots of ways to write expressively, this approach is invaluable. An aesthetic and emotional response to children's work is also needed. Research shows children are very responsive to aesthetic characteristics when they are exposed to them and when those characteristics are noticed in their own work. If a child tells you a story and uses alliteration, violates sequence in order to convey a personal interpretation of an event, or plays with word order in order to evoke vivid images, notice it.

Kenneth Koch, one of the pioneers in teaching creative writing to children, introduced the notion of giving children an opening line or a set of stylistic requirements (for instance, write a poem in which every line must have the name of a color, a proper name, and a food in it). The value of this approach is that the structure frees children to play with the process of writing and directs their attention to the possibilities of form itself. Another way to do this is to read them a great story or poem and suggest they try one in that style.

If a child tells you a story that is about his distant memories of early childhood, you can tell one too. Or ask for another one. Open-endedness, license to tell and write freely, is part of what encourages the development of storytelling, but it is not enough. Children are often deeply social in the way that they approach the task of constructing stories. They need responsive, engaged, attuned listeners and collaborators in order to go on trying to express and create themselves through their stories. To the extent that you see their story as valuable, in both its content and form, they will see it that way too. To the extent that you experience stories of the self as objects for reflection and reworking, they will learn how to do this as well. On the other hand, it is not necessary that your 5-year-old child or student tell the same kind of stories that you tell. They don't need to learn so much how to tell a particular kind of story as to learn that they can tell different types of stories, and that the types they tell affect their audience.

Permit Stories About Things That Matter

It has always struck me that adults like most to read novels about the things that are most gripping to them: poverty and wealth, sex, death, family strife, war, and so on. Yet very often we censor what children tell stories about. One of the first points I tried to make in this book is that form and content are intertwined. The child discovers the form that expresses his meaning. You cannot create or discover exciting or communicative styles and forms if you are not telling a story about something you care about. This means that it should be okay for children to write hate stories, murder stories, sibling revenge stories, stories about sex. Some fear that allowing children to do this might encourage the behavior they write about, or that they are only writing about these things because they watch too much television. Writing about things is itself a kind of action; it doesn't necessarily lead to action. If anything, writing a story about something cools the material.

As to the second concern, kids do mimic TV stories for the same reasons they mimic the storytelling of their parents, siblings, and friends. It is their way of learning their culture. If you want to encourage them to break free of rigid formulas, fine. But perhaps they retell the stories they see on television as a way of gaining mastery over them, exploring them, and understanding them. Viewing the retelling of TV stories in this way shows it in a much more productive light than viewing it as a mind-numbing repetition of mind-numbing material. When a child wants to re-enact or retell a television story, listen to it, ask meaningful questions, and invite him or her to use it as a springboard for invention: Do you want to change the ending? What character would you be? and so on.

I heard two children discussing a film they had just seen, *Last of the Mohicans*. They described, in absorbed and vivid detail, the scene in which a Huron Indian cuts the heart out of his enemy and holds it up. To make it their own, both cognitively and emotionally, they had to make it their own story. Their story of the story seemed to me a lesson in how deeply children experience narratives and how powerful the impulse is to retell, to know narratives through a narrative mode.

We took our son, aged 8, to see a production of *The Taming of the Shrew*. He loved it. The next day I heard him tell the story to two of his friends:

*Well, you see, there was this man. He was sort of like a
government, he was so rich and the boss of everything.
And he had these two daughters. And, you see, in those
days the father decided who his sons and daughters
would marry. And he wanted his older daughter to get
married before his younger daughter. Even though the
younger daughter was much prettier, and nicer and good,
and the older sister was all grumpy and shouting and hit-
ting and very strong, and always beating up her younger
sister and everything. And there was this man who said
he would marry her just because he wanted all the money.
And so after they were married he didn't let her eat or
sleep and he made her walk a long long way, and so she
got weak, and then she finally was good and quiet and
would do what he said. And it was like he had put a spell
over her or something. But then he really fell in love with
her, and at the last minute she broke out of the spell and
was like herself again, but she still loved him.*

This was clearly an integration of what he experienced
watching the play and remembering what I had told him about
the story. But the description of the spell comes directly from
his experience of seeing the performance. In this particular performance, Kate did act as if she were hypnotized when she
delivered her speech of obedience at the end. The way it was
presented (from a contemporary feminist perspective), it was
hard to figure out how Kate could be in love and be so strong-
willed and still deliver a speech like that. Jake did some interpretive work to make sense of it, and he made very good sense
of it at that! In a verbose play with a lot of potentially confusing activity and language (it was presented as a play within a
play), he also kept to the main drama. The meaning of the play
got through to him amidst all the dramatic trappings.

The purpose of encouraging kids to write is not just to get them to write more happily or to become better writers. These experiences have a profound and formative effect on the child's developing narrative voice, and through this, his developing sense of self. The narratives created in writing have a deep connection with the ones created in play and in conversation. These outlets for narrative construction feed one another, and all must be fed by the social and intellectual environment. It is not simply that a kindergartner still needs lots of playtime, or that through play he learns about social roles, negotiating, sorting, and building. Through his play he constructs stories. Casual conversations, playtime, and activities such as sharing anecdotes at dinner or at circle time all contribute to the child's emerging ability to order experiences in a narrative form, express those narratives, and through this process experience himself in new ways. These activities are not reserved for the twenty minutes or so of formal storytelling, they happen throughout the day. They all contribute to the development of the self and to the development of the second world—the one that allows us to live in the past, the future, the impossible, the world of narrative that allows us to share ourselves with others.

Notes

Chapter 1:   The World of Children's Stories

Page 1:   Chapter opening quotation: I learned this quote from my grandmother, Lina Podoloff Derecktor. She attributed it to Johann Wolfgang von Goethe. Although a colleague at Williams, Bruce Kieffer of the German Department, says it sounds as if it might very well be from Goethe, I was unable to locate it.

The story given here, as well as other unattributed examples of children's stories, is taken from my own unpublished data.

Page 4:   Peggy Miller and Lois Sperry, "Early talk about the past: The origins of conversational stories of personal experience," *Journal of Child Language,* 15 (1988), 293–315.

Page 6:   The quotation is from page 35 of Alexander Luria, *Language and Cognition* (New York: Wiley, 1981).

Page 9:   Two books that describe the new interest in stories are Roger Schank, *Tell Me a Story* (New York: Scribner, 1990), and Jerome Bruner, *Actual Minds, Possible Worlds* (Cambridge, MA: Harvard University Press, 1986).

An excellent textbook account of changes in psychological paradigms is found in Charlotte Doyle, *Explorations in Psychology* (Monterey, CA: Brooks-Cole, 1987). See also John Searles's discussion of recent trends in psychology in *The Rediscovery of Mind* (Cambridge, MA: MIT Press, 1992) and Jerome Bruner's discussion in *Acts of Meaning* (Cambridge, MA: Harvard University Press, 1990).

Page 13:   The quotation is found in Luis Buñuel, *My Last Sigh* (New York: Knopf, 1983), page 5.

Page 15: The quotation is from page 94 of Gordon Wells's *The Meaning Makers* (Portsmouth, NH: Heinemann, 1986). Italics are mine.

Page 18: The quotation is from page 28 of Forster's brilliant book, published by Harcourt, Brace in 1927.

Chapter 2: Why Children Tell Stories

Page 24: James Thurber, *The Wonderful O* (New York: Simon & Schuster, 1957).

Page 25: Michael Halliday, *Learning How to Mean* (New York: Elsevier, 1975, 1977).

Page 28: An excellent book that discusses the different ways in which people might mentally categorize objects and concepts is *Cognition and Categorization,* edited by Eleanor Rosch and Barbara Lloyd (Hillsdale, NJ: Lawrence Erlbaum Associates, 1978).

Page 29: The seminal book that describes the original script theory is *Scripts, Plans, Goals and Understanding,* by Roger Schank and Robert Abelson (Hillsdale, NJ: Lawrence Erlbaum Associates, 1977).

A good collection of studies that show how children use routines to organize their knowledge and their language is *Event Knowledge: Structure and Function in Development,* edited by Katherine Nelson (Hillsdale, NJ: Lawrence Erlbaum Associates, 1986).

Page 31: For some older views of children's mental organization, see Jeremy Anglin's *Word Object and Conceptual Development* (New York: Norton, 1977), and Eve Clark's "What's in a word? On the child's acquisition of semantics in his first language." In *Cognitive Development and the Acquisition of Language,* ed. T. E. Moore (New York: Academic Press, 1973), as well as Clark's good account, "Meanings and concepts." In P. E.

Mussen, ed., *Carmichael's Manual of Child Psychology,* Vol. 3, *Cognitive Development,* ed. J. H. Flavell and E. M. Markman (New York: Wiley, 1983), pages 787–840.

Page 32: Emily's monologues, beginning on page 35 and going on through page 39, are found in *Narratives from the Crib,* edited by Katherine Nelson (Cambridge, MA: Harvard University Press, 1989). Quotations are, respectively, from pages 43, 45, and 47.

Page 33: Bruner and Lucariello's comments are from page 76 in the volume *Narratives from the Crib,* edited by Katherine Nelson.

Page 35: See Carol Feldman's essay in *Narratives from the Crib.*

Page 38: Jan Drucker, "The affective context and psychodynamics of first symbolization." In *Symbolic Functioning in Childhood,* ed. N. Smith and M. Franklin (Hillsdale, NJ: Lawrence Erlbaum Associates, 1979).

The psychoanalytic notion of symbols as transitional objects is from a paper presented by the child psychiatrist Eleanor Galenson at the Austen Riggs Center, Stockbridge, MA, March 1992. The topic of the talk was a case study in elective mutism of a little boy.

The importance of transitional objects is discussed by D. W. Winnicott, *Playing and Reality* (London: Tavistock, 1975).

Ulric Neisser talks about different types of self-knowledge in a report called "Five Kinds of Self-Knowledge," published as part of the series *The Emory Cognition Report,* Emory University, September 1988.

Page 40: Annie Dillard, *An American Childhood* (New York: Harper & Row, 1981).

Page 42: Bruno Bettelheim, *The Uses of Enchantment: The Meaning and Importance of Fairy Tales* (New York: Knopf, 1976).

Jason's experiences are detailed in Vivian Paley's *The Boy Who Would Be a Helicopter* (Cambridge, MA: Harvard

University Press, 1990).

Page 46: Shirley Brice Heath, *Ways with Words* (Cambridge: Cambridge University Press, 1983).

Hadyn White, "The value of narrativity in the representation of reality." In *Critical Inquiry on Narrative,* ed. W. J. T. Mitchell, vol. 7, no. 1 (1980), and vol. 7, no. 4 (1981). This is a wonderful collection of papers that draws together a wide array of theoretical perspectives on narrative.

Page 47: Experiments on memory: Frederic C. Bartlett, *Remembering* (Cambridge: Cambridge University Press, 1932).

How to tell the right kind of story: Sarah Michaels, "The dismantling of narrative." In *Developing Narrative Structure,* ed. Carole Peterson and Allyssa McCabe (Hillsdale, NJ: Lawrence Erlbaum Associates, 1991).

Page 49: The essay by Paul Ricoeur is "A model of the text: Meaningful action considered as a text." In *The Interpretive Social Science: A Reader,* ed. Paul Rabinow and William Sullivan (Berkeley: University of California Press, 1979).

The speech act idea is discussed by J. L. Austin in *How to Do Things with Words* (New York: Oxford University Press, 1962), and by John Searle in *Speech Acts* (Cambridge: Cambridge University Press, 1970).

Page 51: See Gordon Wells's *The Meaning Makers* (Portsmouth, NH: Heinemann, 1986).

Ways in which children establish and maintain feelings of intimacy through storytelling: "Wanna be lucky and have two cameras? Friendship and collaborative narration in preschool," honors thesis written by Eileen Anderson, under my supervision, Williams College, 1993.

Page 55: For Neisser's thoughts on constructing an extended self, see his "Five Kinds of Self-Knowledge."

Chapter 3: Perspectives on Narratives

Page 59: The chapter's opening quotation is from Charles Dickens,

David Copperfield (New York: Heritage Press, 1937), page 1.

Page 60: Samuel Levin, in his book *Metaphoric Worlds* (New Haven, CT: Yale University Press, 1988), argues that every poem begins with an invisible invitation that frames one's interpretation of the poem; see also "Concerning what kind of speech act a poem is." In *Pragmatics of Language and Literature,* ed. Tevn A. van Dijk (Amsterdam: North Holland, 1976).

The quotation is on page 79 in *The Pear Stories: Cultural, Cognitive and Linguistic Aspects of Narrative Production,* ed. Wallace Chafe (Norwood, NJ: Ablex, 1980).

Page 61: See Chafe's *Pear Stories.* Nancy Stein presented a paper, "A model of storytelling skills," at the Boston University Conference on Language Development in October 1986. She also contributed "The development of children's storytelling skills" to *Child Language: A Reader,* ed. M. Franklin and S. Barten (New York: Oxford University Press, 1988). For Allyssa McCabe's work, see, for instance, Carole Peterson and Allyssa McCabe, eds., *Developing Narrative Structure* (Hillsdale, NJ: Lawrence Erlbaum Associates, 1991). Also relevant here is Michael Bamberg, "Action, events, scenes, plots and the drama," and "Language and the constitution of part-whole relationships," *Language Sciences* (1994), 1–41.

Three books that focus on clinical interpretations and uses of people's life stories are *Retelling a Life* by Roy Schafer (New York: Basic Books, 1992), *Narratives and the Self* by Anthony Kerby (Bloomington: Indiana University Press, 1991), and *Narrative Truth and Historical Truth* by Donald Spence (New York: Norton, 1982).

The process of storytelling itself: Charlotte Doyle, "Motivations of young authors: Why did Rachel tell so many stories?" Paper presented at the annual convention of the American Psychological Association, Boston, 1990.

Page 62: The quotation is found on page 5 in Barbara Biber's *Early Education and Psychological Development* (New Haven, CT: Yale University Press, 1984).

Page 63: Two good books that represent some of the best work on computer models of children's cognitive development are *Children's Thinking: What Develops?* ed. Robert Siegler (Hillsdale, NJ: Lawrence Erlbaum Associates, 1978), and *Information Processing in Children,* ed. Sylvia Farnham Diggory (New York: Academic Press, 1972).

Pages 64–65: Judy Hudson, Janet Gebelt, Jeanette Haviland, and Christina Bentivegna, "Emotion and narrative structure in young children's personal accounts," *Journal of Narrative and Life History,* 2(2) (1992), 129–159. See also Robyn Fivush, "Exploring sex differences in the emotional content of mother-child conversations about the past," *Sex Roles,* 20(11/12) (1989), 675–691. Christine Todd reported on this study in a symposium, "Learning to talk about the past," at the Conference on Human Development, Nashville, TN, April 1986.

Page 65: Some research has attempted to separate issues of content from issues of form and content. This is in order to examine with more control and certainty aspects of structure and cognitive changes manifested in storytelling. The material or stimuli in these kinds of studies are stories the researcher has chosen usually as much for their transparent and manipulable structure as for their emotional impact or relevance to the particular children participating in the study. Script studies, for example, use stories about an event chosen by the experimenter for its blandness and its routine quality rather than for its individual meaning to the child. In any given study, then, there may be something of a trade-off between the kind of control of material that allows for precise and evenhanded analyses and the use of material that is personally meaningful, spontaneously produced, idiosyncratic (and therefore true to life), but also somewhat less amenable to tight measures and analyses. Stories that are laden with affect may be harder to collect and analyze than less personally relevant stories, told in more neutral situations, but are nonetheless essential to understand.

A good discussion of young children's memory for real events is in Christine Todd and Marion Perlmutter, "Reality recalled by preschool children." In *New Directions for Children's Development: Children's Memory,* no. 10 (San Francisco: Jossey-Bass, 1980).

Everything said is not a story: Robert Russel and Joan Lucariello, "Narrative, yes. Narrative ad infinitum, no!" *American Psychologist,* May 1992.

Page 67: On linguistic interaction: James Britton, *Language and Learning* (London: Penguin, 1970), and Arthur Applebee, *The Child's Conception of Story* (Chicago: University of Chicago Press, 1978).

Page 68: On logic and poetry: Suzanne Langer, *Feeling and Form* (London: Routledge & Kegan Paul, 1953).

For his distinction, see Jerome Bruner, *Actual Minds, Possible Worlds* (Cambridge, MA: Harvard University Press, 1986).

Page 70: For Bruner's criteria for a narrative, see Jerome Bruner and Joan Lucariello, in *Narratives from the Crib,* ed. Katherine Nelson (Cambridge, MA: Harvard University Press, 1989).

Page 73: Sequence coupled with meaning: See Bruner's *Actual Minds, Possible Worlds.* See also his *Acts of Meaning* (Cambridge, MA: Harvard University Press, 1990).

Page 76: For Barbara Rogoff's research, see in particular her *Apprenticeship in Thinking: Cognitive Development in a Social Context* (New York: Oxford University Press, 1990).

Page 77: The quotation is from page 3 of "Girl," by Jamaica Kincaid, in a collection of her stories, *At the Bottom of the River* (New York: Farrar, Straus and Giroux, 1978).

Page 78: Tsetevan Todorov, *Genres in Discourse* (New York: Cambridge University Press, 1990). Another interesting book on the relationship between reader and writer in creating the meaning of a text is Wolfgang Iser's *The Act of Reading* (Baltimore: Johns Hopkins University Press, 1978).

One common criterion for what makes something narrative is that it contain some sense of events unfolding in time. Todorov talks about this in a particularly rich way. A narrative, he says, must not only be situated in time, it must slice time up into discontinuous units. In addition, a narrative must present the "unfolding of an action, change, difference" (*Genres in Discourse,* page 28). A narrative must also include "a formative transformation." This refers to something that happens, some state or situation that changes or is changed in the body of the text. A transformation can also be evocative rather than formative. In this case the transformation occurs in the mind of the reader, rather than being explicitly stated or described in the text.

Another seminal discussion of the relationship between the unfolding of events and their representation in narratives is in Paul Ricoeur's *Time and Narrative* (Chicago: University of Chicago Press, 1984).

Chapter 4: The Kinds of Stories Children Tell

Page 84:   P. J. Miller and L. L. Sperry, "Early talk about the past: The origins of conversational stories of personal experience," *Journal of Child Language,* 15 (1988), 293–316. See also P. J. Miller and B. Byhouwer, "The acquisition of culture through stories of personal experience," paper presented at the symposium "The Acquisition of Culture Through Talk," meeting of the American Ethnological Society, San Antonio, TX, 1987.

These findings were described in my dissertation, "Learning to reminisce: A developmental study of how young children talk about the past," City University of New York Graduate School, 1985.

Alison Preece, "The range of narrative forms conversationally produced by young children," *Journal of Child Language,* 14 (1987), 353–373.

Page 86:   William Labov presents the best discussion of the role of commentary in directing how a narrative should be heard in an article he wrote with Joshua Waletsky, "Narrative analysis: Oral versions of personal experience." In *Essays in the Verbal and Visual Arts,* ed. J. Helms (Seattle: University of Washington Press, 1967), pages 12–44.

Page 88: These results were presented in papers that were part of a symposium on "Learning to Talk About the Past," Conference on Human Development, with Marion Perlmutter, Christine Todd, Susan Engel, Judy Hudson, and Robyn Fivush, Nashville, TN, April 1986.

Page 96: The quotations are on pages 67 and 73 of Virginia Woolf, *Moments of Being* (New York: Harcourt, Brace, 1976).

Karen Malan, "Structure and coherence in South African children's personal narratives," paper presented at the Boston University Conference on Language Development, Boston, October 1992.

Page 97: Judy Dunn, *The Beginnings of Social Understanding* (Cambridge, MA: Harvard University Press, 1988).

Page 99: Elizabeth Loftus, "The reality of repressed memories," *American Psychologist,* 48(5) (May 1993), 518–537.

Page 100: Gordon Wells, *The Meaning Makers* (Portsmouth, NH: Heinemann, 1986).

Page 104: See page 107 of Wells's *Meaning Makers.*

The quoted passage is found on pages 13–14 of Jonathan Kozol's *Savage Inequalities* (New York: Crown, 1991).

Page 108: Stoel-Gammon and Scliar-Cabral, "Learning how to tell it like it is: The development of the reportive function in children's speech." In *Papers and Reports on Child Language Development* (Stanford, CA: Stanford University Press, 1977).

Page 109: Vivian Paley, *The Boy Who Would Be a Helicopter* (Cambridge, MA: Harvard University Press, 1990).

Nancy Stein and Tom Trabasso discuss the formal nature of a story in "What's in a story?" which appears in a collection edited by R. Glaser entitled *Advances in Instructional Psychology,* Vol. 2, pages 213–267 (Hillsdale, NJ: Lawrence Erlbaum

Associates, 1982).

Page 110:   Carol Feldman, "Genres as mental models," paper presented at the Instituto de Filosofia, Naples, November 1989.

Chapter 5: The Origins of Storytelling

Page 114:   Catherine Snow, "Mother's speech research: From input to interaction." In *Talking to Children,* ed. Catherine Snow and Charles Ferguson (Cambridge: Cambridge University Press, 1977).

Jerome Bruner, on scaffolding: "The ontogenesis of speech acts," *Journal of Child Language,* 2 (1975), 1–21. See also "The decontextualization of word meanings within an event context" by Katherine Nelson, Susan Engel, and Amy Kyratzis, *Journal of Pragmatics,* special issue, 1985.

Page 116:   Grace de Laguna, *Speech, Its Function and Development* (New Haven, CT: Yale University Press, 1972); Heinz Werner, *The Comparative Psychology of Mental Development* (New York: International Universities Press, 1973); Catherine Snow and C. Ferguson, eds., *Talking to Children* (Cambridge: Cambridge University Press, 1977); Roger Brown, *A First Language* (Cambridge, MA: Harvard University Press, 1973); Jacqueline Sachs, "Talk about the there and then." In *Children's Language,* Vol. 4, ed. Keith Nelson (New York: Gardner Press, 1983). See also Judy Deloache, "Joint picture book reading as memory training for toddlers," paper presented at the Society for Research in Child Development, Detroit, April 1983; Susan Engel, Amy Kyratzis, and Joan Lucariello, "Early past and future talk in a social interactive context," paper presented at the Memory Development and the Development of Memory Talk Symposium conducted at the Infancy Conference, New York, 1984. Sachs also discusses maternal scaffolding in "Talk about the there and then."

Page 118: Colwyn Trevarthen, "The foundations of intersubjectivity: Development of interpersonal and cooperative understanding in infants." In *The Social Foundations of Language and Thought,* ed. D. Olsen (New York: Norton, 1980).

Page 119: Sachs, "Talk about the there and then." A good study describing the relationship of children's memory to context is by Joan Lucariello and Katherine Nelson, "Situational variation in mother-child interactions," paper presented at the meeting of the Third International Conference on Infant Studies, Austin, TX, March 1982.

Page 121: Deloache, "Joint picture book reading."

Page 122: Bambi Scheifflin, "Getting it together: An ethnographic approach to the study of the development of communicative competence." In *Developmental Pragmatics,* ed. E. Ochs and B. Scheifflin (New York: Academic Press, 1979).

Ann Eisenberg, "Learning to describe past experiences in conversation," *Discourse Processes,* 8 (1985), 177–204.

Mary Mullen, "Earliest recollections of childhood and mother-child talk about past events," doctoral dissertation, Harvard University, 1993.

Page 123: Frederic C. Bartlett, *Remembering* (Cambridge: Cambridge University Press, 1932).

Page 124: Lev Vygotsky, *Mind in Society* (Cambridge, MA: Harvard University Press, 1978); Barbara Rogoff and Jean Lave, eds., *Everyday Cognition* (Cambridge, MA: Harvard University Press, 1984); James Wertsch, *Vygotsky and the Social Formation of Mind* (Cambridge, MA: Harvard University Press, 1985).

Page 125: The quotation is found on page 50 of Irving Sigel and Luis Laosa's *Families as Learning Environments* (New York: Plenum Press, 1982).

On parent and child co-construction: Ronald Scollon, "A real early stage: An unzipped condensation of a dissertation on child language." In *Developmental Pragmatics,* ed. E. Ochs and B. Scheifflin (New York: Academic Press, 1979).

Page 126: The idea that social interactions are where we will find children talking about the past is excellently presented in Hillary Horn Ratner's "The role of social context in memory development." In *Children's Memory: New Directions for Child Development,* no. 10, ed. Marion Perlmutter (San Francisco: Jossey-Bass, 1980).

Page 143: I reported on the research on the remembering styles of preschoolers in a paper "Are there reminiscers and practical rememberers in the classroom?" Boston University Conference on Language Development, Boston, October 1992.

Page 145: Alison Preece, "Critics and collaborators and critics: The nature and effect of peer interaction on children's conversational narratives," *Journal of Narrative and Life History,* 2(3) (1992), 277–292.

Shirley Brice Heath, *Ways with Words* (Cambridge: Cambridge University Press, 1983). The quotations are taken from pages 294–295.

Chapter 6: Developing a Narrative Voice

Page 151: The quotation is taken from pages 287–288 of *The Essays of George Eliot,* ed. Thomas Pinney (London: Routledge & Kegan Paul, 1963).

Page 153: Shirley Brice Heath, *Ways with Words* (Cambridge: Cambridge University Press, 1983).

Page 156: Claudia Lewis, "Creative experience and language." In *Dimensions of Language Experience,* ed. C. Winsor (New York: Agathon Press, 1975).

In "How to tell a good story: The intersection of language and affect in children's narratives," *Journal of Narrative and Life History,* 2(4) (1992), 355–376, Judy Snitzer Reilly looks at how children use paralinguistic devices in telling their stories and gives evidence for Lewis's point. For a different perspective, see Justine

Cassell and David MacNeil, "Gesture and the poetics of prose," *Poetics Today,* 12(3) (Fall 1991), 375–404.

Page 158: Two excellent papers on the function of a telos in theory and research on child development are Bernard Kaplan's "Genetic dramatism: Old wine in new bottles" and Joe Glick's "Piaget, Vygotsky and Werner." Both are in *Toward a Holistic Developmental Psychology,* ed. S. Wapner and B. Kaplan (Hillsdale, NJ: Lawrence Erlbaum Associates, 1983).

Page 161: Anthony Pelligrini and Lee Galda, "The joint construction of stories by preschool children and an experimenter." In *Narrative Thought and Narrative Language,* ed. B. Britton and A. Pellegrini (Hillsdale, NJ: Lawrence Erlbaum Associates, 1990). The quotation is from page 125.

Page 163: Gillian McNamee, "The social interaction origins of narrative skills," *Quarterly Newsletter of the Laboratory of Comparative Human Cognition,* October 1979, pages 63–68.

Page 164: Allyssa McCabe and Carole Peterson, "Getting the story: A longitudinal study of parental styles in eliciting narratives and development of narrative skill." In *Developing Narrative Structure,* ed. Allyssa McCabe and Carole Peterson (Hillsdale, NJ: Lawrence Erlbaum Associates, 1991). The quotations are from pages 238 and 242.

Page 166: Bruner discusses this notion in a book he wrote with the help of Rita Watson called *A Child's Talk: Learning to Use Language* (New York: Norton, 1983); and Catherine Snow discusses it in "The development of conversation between mothers and babies," *Journal of Child Language,* 4 (1977), 1–22. In contrast, see Sarah Michaels, "The dismantling of narrative." In *Developing Narrative Structure,* ed. A. McCabe and C. Peterson (Hillsdale, NJ: Lawrence Erlbaum Associates, 1991).

Page 169: The opening quotation is from E. B. White's essay "The living language," in *Writings from the New Yorker,* ed. Rebecca Dale (New York: HarperCollins, 1990), page 143.

Carol Feldman, "Genres as mental models," paper presented at the Instituto de Filosofia, Naples, November 1989.

Page 172: Mikhail Bakhtin, *The Problem of Dostoevsky's Poetics* (Minneapolis: University of Minnesota Press, 1984); James Wertsch, *Voices of the Mind* (Cambridge, MA: Harvard University Press, 1991); and John Dore, personal communication, professor of developmental psychology, CUNY Graduate Center, New York.

Page 173: Annie Dillard, *An American Childhood* (New York: Harper & Row, 1987).

Pages 174–175: James Gee calls for a recognition of the poetic in children's narratives. See his "Memory and myth." In *Developing Narrative Structure,* ed. A. McCabe and C. Peterson (Hillsdale, NJ: Lawrence Erlbaum Associates, 1991).

Page 176: William Carlos Williams, *The Collected Poems of William Carlos Williams, 1909–1939, vol. I* (New York: New Directions, 1985).

Chapter 7: We Are the Stories We Tell

Page 183: The chapter's opening quotation is from Patricia Hampl, *A Romantic Education* (Boston: Houghton Mifflin, 1982), pages 5–6.

Page 185: Ulric Neisser, "Five kinds of self-knowledge," *Philosophical Psychology,* 1 (1988), 35–59.

Page 186: The discussion is taken from Chapter 3, "The self," of William James's *Psychology: The Briefer Course* (New York: Henry Holt, 1910).

Page 187: Roy Schafer, *Retelling a Life* (New York: Basic Books, 1992).

Page 188: Vladimir Nabakov, *Speak, Memory* (New York:

Random House, 1967). The quotation on page 189 is from pages 46–47. See Dan McAdams, *The Stories We Live By: Personal Myths and the Making of the Self* (New York: Morrow, 1993). See also Erik Erikson, *Childhood and Society* (New York: Norton, 1950).

Page 195: Peggy Miller, Judith Mintz, Lisa Hoogstra, Heidi Fong, and Randolph Potts, "The narrated self: Young children's construction of self in relation to others in conversational stories of personal experience," *Merrill Palmer Quarterly,* 38(1) (1992), 45–67.

Page 200: Carolyn Steedman presents this remarkable story and her analysis of it in *The Tidy House: Little Girls' Writing* (London: Virago Press, 1982).

Chapter 8: Fostering Narrative Development

Page 217: Donald Graves, *Writing: Teachers and Children at Work* (Exeter, NH: Heinemann, 1983).

Kenneth Koch, *Rose, Where Did You Get That Red? Teaching Great Poetry to Children* (New York: Random House, 1973).

Index